# THE MANAGEMENT OF INNOVATION

ALBERTO GALASSO

# The Management of Innovation

## Managing and Creating Technology Capital

UNIVERSITY OF TORONTO PRESS
Toronto Buffalo London

Rotman-UTP Publishing
An imprint of University of Toronto Press
Toronto  Buffalo  London
utorontopress.com
© University of Toronto Press 2024

**Library and Archives Canada Cataloguing in Publication**

Title: The management of innovation : managing and creating technology capital / Alberto Galasso.
Names: Galasso, Alberto, author.
Description: Includes bibliographical references and index.
Identifiers: Canadiana (print) 20240282590 | Canadiana (ebook) 20240282612 | ISBN 9781487553562 (cloth) | ISBN 9781487553593 (EPUB) | ISBN 9781487553579 (PDF)
Subjects: LCSH: Technological innovations – Management.
Classification: LCC HD45 .G35 2024 | DDC 658.4/063 – dc23

ISBN 978-1-4875-5356-2 (cloth)        ISBN 978-1-4875-5359-3 (EPUB)
                                       ISBN 978-1-4875-5357-9 (PDF)

Cover design: Will Brown

We wish to acknowledge the land on which the University of Toronto Press operates. This land is the traditional territory of the Wendat, the Anishnaabeg, the Haudenosaunee, the Métis, and the Mississaugas of the Credit First Nation.

University of Toronto Press acknowledges the financial support of the Government of Canada and the Ontario Arts Council, an agency of the Government of Ontario, for its publishing activities.

ONTARIO ARTS COUNCIL
CONSEIL DES ARTS DE L'ONTARIO
an Ontario government agency
un organisme du gouvernement de l'Ontario

Funded by the    Financé par le
Government    gouvernement
of Canada        du Canada        | Canadä

*A Flavio e Francesca*

# Contents

# Acknowledgments

During the years required to write this book, I incurred many debts. Without doubt, my biggest debt is to the hundreds of students who attended my lectures on innovation and technology management. They are the main reason why I embarked on this project.

At the same time, the book builds heavily on the ideas (and occasionally the writing) developed in several research projects that I published in the past decade. These include research articles with Ajay Agrawal, Iain Cockburn, Stefano Comino, Clara Graziano, Hong Luo, Matthew Mitchell, Alexander Oettl, Carlos Serrano, Timothy Simcoe, Mihkel Tombak, Gabor Virag, and Rosemarie Ziedonis. Working with these scholars is a pleasure and a rewarding learning experience. Special thanks go to Mark Schankerman, my coauthor and former PhD advisor at the London School of Economics, who sparked my interest in the field of economics of innovation.

My thinking on the topics covered in this book was also influenced by conversations with supportive colleagues at the Rotman School of Management of the University of Toronto, including Kevin Bryan, El Hadi Caoui, Ruben Gaetani, Joshua Gans, Nicola Lacetera, Anita McGahan, and the late Will Mitchell.

Sarina Gill provided excellent research assistance on the empirical analysis presented in the Appendix. I also benefited from constructive comments from many readers of the working drafts. In particular, I would like to thank Fiona Bai, Patrick Bedford, Darya Ivantsova, Shirley Li, and Emilia Mah.

Several of the chapters in this book were taught as part of Technology Strategy, Strategic Management, and Prices and Markets courses at the MBA, the Master of Management of Innovation, and the Commerce programs offered by the University of Toronto.

I also would like to thank Karen Temple, Jennifer Fraser, and Tamara O'Connell at the Innovations and Partnerships Office of the University of Toronto for their help and guidance on the use of patent documents in this book.

I am indebted to Jennifer DiDomenico, editorial director at the University of Toronto Press, for believing in this project and for her support and guidance during the writing and publishing processes. Mary Lui and Susan Bindernagel provided excellent managing editorial and editing support.

The final thanks go to my wife Adrina and my two children Sebastian and Catherine. I could not have completed this work without their love, encouragement, and support.

Toronto, Ontario

# Introduction

*It's not enough what I did in the past – there is also the future.*

– Rita Levi-Montalcini[1]

One billion dollars is a lot of money. With that kind of money, one can buy a private island in the Bahamas or the Miami Marlins baseball team. It is not surprising, then, that the business and technology worlds were rocked when, in August 2012, a court in California awarded Apple more than one billion dollars in damages over claims that Samsung had copied the Apple iPhone and iPad tablet technologies. And that was just the beginning.

The Apple-Samsung patent battle, which began in 2011, continued for seven long years. The two companies sued and countersued each other many times, judicial decisions were appealed, and the case even reached the US Supreme Court. Before reaching a settlement in 2018, Apple released the following statement:

> *This case has always been about more than money. Apple ignited the smartphone revolution with iPhone and it is a fact that Samsung blatantly copied our design. It is important that we continue to protect the hard work and innovation of so many people at Apple.*

The statement captures well the aggressive stance taken by Apple – a stance that began with Apple CEO Steve Jobs's decision to conduct a "thermonuclear war" against technology companies running the Android operating system on their devices.[2]

Things do not have to be so tense in every technology interaction. In many cases, innovators are willing to share their technologies with other firms and easily reach agreements on how to do so. Take for example the case of Genentech, a company founded in 1976 by venture capitalist Robert Swanson and University of California Professor Herbert Boyer. Genentech scientists were the first to synthetize human insulin. This discovery ended an intense race against other academic research labs and attracted the attention of the major pharmaceutical company Eli Lilly. Genentech and Eli Lilly quickly negotiated an exclusive licensing deal. Eli Lilly obtained the rights to manufacture and market the insulin; Genentech obtained royalties on sales and funds to conduct further research.

The Genentech–Eli Lilly agreement was the first of its kind. Never before had a large pharmaceutical company relied on the proprietary research of a small for-profit startup. The industry quickly discovered that this arrangement was a win-win. It allowed small new firms to pursue cutting edge research without worrying about the large financial resources needed to commercialize and develop a new drug. At the same time, this arrangement allowed large pharmaceutical companies to tap into external technologies rather than rely only on their internal research pipeline. This, indeed, was the licensing deal that opened the field for a new industry: biotech. Since then, such contractual agreements between established pharmaceutical firms and biotech ventures have become the industry norm.

Firms may even decide to share their technologies with third parties without relying on contracts at all. This is, for example, what American electric vehicle and clean energy company Tesla decided to do. In June 2014, CEO Elon Musk released a statement titled *All*

*Our Patent Are Belong to You*, announcing that Tesla was no longer enforcing intellectual property (IP).[3]

> *Yesterday, there was a wall of Tesla patents in the lobby of our Palo Alto headquarters. That is no longer the case. They have been removed, in the spirit of the open source movement, for the advancement of electric vehicle technology.*

So the statement read, and it continued, explaining how firms in the industry could freely use Tesla technologies without worrying about patent lawsuits from the company.

Synthetic insulin, smartphones, and electric cars are all important technologies that required substantial research investments and years of work to be developed. Creating these technologies requires understanding the latest scientific knowledge, hiring the right talent pool, and building an organizational structure that incentivizes experimentation, discovery, and innovation. But the lesson from these three stories is that creation of the technology is only the first step. Firms also need to decide how to manage their technologies. This requires deciding what to protect, what to share, and how to share it. Apple, Genentech, and Tesla followed very different approaches for their technologies. Identifying the options and picking the right technology management strategy can be as hard as creating the technology in the first place.

*The Management of Innovation* examines how firms can leverage and create technology capital. Despite the importance of innovation for the growth of firms, industries, and national economies, the process by which firms innovate and the strategic tools available to effectively manage new technologies are often neglected by entrepreneurs, corporate managers, and policymakers.

Over the past two decades, economists and management scholars have developed several new insights on how companies can be more innovative. Many of these research findings have the potential to be very useful for technology startups and corporations, but they have not yet reached management practice. The technical nature of the academic economics and management literature often makes these studies not easily accessible to scientists and engineers. *The Management of Innovation* aims to facilitate access to this knowledge by providing an introduction to the latest research in the innovation literature for non-specialists.

The analysis considers the two key stages of the innovation process: technology management and technology creation. Deciding how to allocate resources and managerial attention between these two stages is difficult. Each stage is complex and multifaceted. This book examines the most frequent trade-offs that shape the innovation process across these two stages. It also discusses the most effective tools that firms can use to manage and create new technologies. As suggested by Rita Levi-Montalcini in the epigraph, the process is fully dynamic. The way a firm manages the technology capital it created in the past affects its ability to develop future technologies. These insights can help startup entrepreneurs and corporate managers alike to avoid making poor decisions.

The first part of the book focuses on technology management. Its central theme is a discussion of how firms can leverage their technologies with IP, such as patents, copyrights, and trademarks. This part of the book begins with an introduction to IP for managers and entrepreneurs. It covers the historical origin of IP and its economic foundation; it also discusses the key managerial and economic trade-offs generated by IP identified in the academic literature. The book then provides a guide to the patenting process, describing the key steps that inventors need to follow to obtain national and international patents.

The analysis combines practical information and academic insights into how patent examination can impact firms' profits and shape their strategies. It discusses the ways in which firms can use patents to protect and share their technologies and provides an overview of the latest research on patent litigation and patent licensing. This part of the book also introduces the reader to patent analytics, that is, the use of patent data to examine the technological landscape in which a firm operates and to predict new technology trends.

Patent analytics has been overlooked by academic texts and more popular business books on technological innovation. *The Management of Innovation* aims to change that. In the past few years, several free online portals (such as Google Patent Search™ service) have emerged.[4] These portals allow managers to conduct simple patent analytics studies without the need for sophisticated statistical knowledge or special software packages. Learning how to collect and examine these patent data will be particularly helpful to technology startups and small firms that often do not have the resources to hire external consultants.

During the past decade, I have engaged heavily in the world of technology startups. I have advised several ventures through the Creative Destruction Lab, the leading Canadian program for massively scalable, seed-stage, science- and technology-based companies. Performing a patent landscape analysis has been a crucial requirement for many of these ventures to convince investors of the uniqueness of their technologies and to better understand their competition. *The Management of Innovation* provides an introduction to several simple techniques that can be used to guide this analysis.

The second part of the book focuses on technology creation. Its central theme is an examination of the drivers of innovation inside and outside the firm. This part of the book covers how a firm can leverage the crowd as an innovation partner through an open-innovation strategy. It also discusses the power of incentives to shape the behavior of scientists and innovators. It provides an analysis of a rich array of insights, which the academic literature has developed, into how the local environment in which a firm operates shapes innovation activity. The book concludes with a discussion of how customer and employee safety can have a profound impact on a firm's innovation.

The analysis of the link between product safety and technology strategy is another key difference between *The Management of Innovation* and existing books on technology management. Despite the importance of health and safety, the voluminous business literature on innovation has neglected the role that technology plays in avoiding dangerous product failures. My ongoing research agenda with Hong Luo aims to address this gap. This book summarizes new insights from our work on why technology managers should pay attention to product liability risk and on how a firm's technology strategy should change in the case of a prominent product failure.

# PART 1

# TECHNOLOGY MANAGEMENT

# CHAPTER 1

# Intellectual Property

*Intellectual property is the oil of the 21st century.*

– Mark Getty[1]

## 1.1 Intellectual Property

In a 2004 interview for the *Chief Executive* magazine, Microsoft Chairman Bill Gates stated that

> *over the last 10 years, it has become imperative for CEOs to have not just a general understanding of the intellectual property issues facing their business and their industry, but to have quite a refined expertise relating to those issues. … it is no longer simply the legal department's problem. CEOs must now be able to formulate strategies that capitalize on and maximize the value of their company's intellectual property assets to drive growth, innovation and cooperative relationships with other companies.[2]*

Gates's intuition proved correct. In fact, current estimates suggest that more than 85 percent of the S&P500 market value is linked not to traditional tangible assets such as land, buildings, or manufacturing equipment but instead to intangible assets.[3] Intellectual property (IP), as emphasized by Bill Gates, and also Mark Getty as seen in the epigraph, is one of the most important intangible assets.

But what is IP? William Landes and Richard Posner, two lead-ing figures in the academic field of law and economics, defined IP rights as

*legal regimes of property rights covering ideas, inventions, discoveries, sym-bols, images, expressive works (verbal, visual, musical, theatrical) and other potentially valuable human products (broadly, "information") that have an existence separable from a unique physical embodiment.*[4]

New technologies – such as a new type of smartphone or a new car engine – are essentially a combination of tangible components and intangible knowledge related to the design and manufactur-ing processes. Consider, for example, developing a new model of musical instrument, such as a new type of saxophone. You may go through various attempts to develop a new woodwind instrument until you obtain a saxophone that differs from existing models in terms of design, materials, or other aspects of the technical per-formance. The process may lead you to develop a complete proto-type of the new saxophone that you can play and show to people. Notice that the value of the new instrument is not limited to the value of the physical components that comprise the prototype (e.g., the bell, the body, and the neck). The value also extends to the knowledge that you possess on how to develop this new type of saxophone, the information that you have on the inputs and components that need to be used, and your knowledge of the right way to combine them.

Intellectual property (IP) refers to property rights on this intangi-ble knowledge underlying an innovation. IP defines the boundaries of the protected knowledge and identifies the owner of such infor-mation. As I will discuss below and in later chapters of the book, the economic issues associated with property rights on knowledge are somewhat different from those related to traditional property rights on tangible assets, such as the ownership of houses or cars.

Essentially all countries around the world provide some form of IP rights. These rights are so important that they were recognized by the Universal Declaration of Human Rights proclaimed by the United Nations General Assembly in Paris in 1948. This declaration listed 30 rights and freedoms that everybody across the world is expected to enjoy. They include freedom from torture and the right to freedom of opinion. Article 27 of this declaration states that

> *everyone has the right to the protection of the moral and material interests resulting from any scientific, literary or artistic production of which s/he is the author.*

Intellectual property rights are often divided into two broad categories. The first is industrial property, which includes patents, trademarks, and industrial designs. The second category is copyright, which covers literary work, movies, music, and other forms of creative artistic work.

Patents are a very important form of IP. They provide property rights on inventions related to new products or processes. A patent owner (technically called the "patentee") has the exclusive right to stop others from making, using, selling, or importing products or processes based on the patented invention. Patentees can enforce their patents against infringement taking place in the country that granted the patent. Patent protection lasts for a specific time, which is typically twenty years from the date the patent application was filed at the patent office. When the patent term expires, the technology becomes freely available.

As the quote from Bill Gates indicates, the development of an effective technology strategy requires a solid understanding of the nature of the various forms of IP rights. Startups and large firms often develop IP strategies to prevent third parties from appropriating their technical knowledge, to regulate access to their technologies, and to generate returns from their scientific discoveries. I will discuss these issues at length in this book. Before beginning with this analysis, in the next sections I provide a brief overview of the history of patents and discuss their economic foundation.

## 1.2  History of Patents

In medieval Europe, the Latin term *litterae clausae* denoted sealed royal letters. Conversely, the term *litterae patentes* referred to open royal letters and is believed to be the probable source of the modern term "patents."[5]

Medieval monarchs awarded monopoly rights to their most loyal supporters over mineral extractions or over the production and commercialization of particular goods. These patents were given at the discretion of the ruler and were not necessarily linked to new technologies. The first example of a patent system open to the public, in which all inventors could submit applications and the novelty of the technology was assessed by an external body, was established in Renaissance Venice in 1474. The law enacting this system, the Venetian Patent Act, has been recognized by numerous historians and law scholars as the legal foundation of modern patent systems.[6]

As detailed in a study that I conducted with Stefano Comino and Clara Graziano, in the Republic of Venice, which corresponds to modern north-east Italy, the process of patenting involved different steps. Patent applications were granted after approval from the Senate. The subject matter to be patented was required to be a *new and ingenious device*, and this novelty content was evaluated on the basis of the technologies used in the Republic of Venice, implying that a patent could be granted to products or processes already available elsewhere. The Venetian Patent Act stated that the effect of a patent was to stop *every other person in any of our territories and towns to make any further device conforming with and similar to said one without the consent and license of the author*. This wording is very similar to the modern patent laws that are implemented around the world.[7]

In subsequent centuries, patent law spread across Europe. In 1623, the English Parliament passed the Statute of Monopolies, which provides the foundation of the modern British patent system. Economist Erich Kaufer suggests that the duration of British patents was set to fourteen years to approximate the time needed to train two generations of apprentices (seven years per apprentice term).[8] France implemented a patent law in 1791.

The British Colonies in North America passed patent laws in the seventeenth century, which were inspired by the British system. Prominent examples of these laws are those of Massachusetts (1641), Connecticut (1672), and South Carolina (1784).

The first US federal patent law was promulgated in 1790. Since then, the US patent office has granted more than 11 million patents covering some of the most important innovations in modern history. The list of famous US patents is long and fascinating, encompassing many impactful technologies that changed the world. Examples include the telephone patent granted to Alexander Graham Bell in 1876 (patent US 174,465); the PageRank patent by Google's co-founder Larry Page in 2001 (patent US 6,285,999) and the mRNA COVID-19 vaccine patent by Moderna's inventors Giuseppe Ciaramella and Sunny Himansu in 2021 (patent US 10,702,600).

The first Canadian patent was granted by the legislature of Quebec in 1791. Canadian patents were granted for five years but could be renewed for two additional five-year periods.[9]

The Republic of Venice was also the first European country to grant book privileges, which allowed authors and publishers to control printing and sales of their books. This took place in the early days of the publishing industry, following the development of the first movable-type press in Mainz, Germany, by Johannes Gutenberg in 1447. These book privileges are the antecedents of modern copyright laws. Interestingly, the development of this early form of copyright was driven by concerns of monarchs and religious authorities over the spread of libelous and heretical writings. By giving authors control over the circulation of their books, the copyright provision reduced the incentives to publish anonymously subversive and heretical books.[10]

## 1.3 The Economic Foundation of Patents

Patents give their owners property rights over the protected invention for a pre-determined period of time. More specifically, patentees can exclude other firms and individuals from making, using, selling, or importing the patented inventions without their permission. From an economic perspective, the patent grants the patentee temporary monopoly power because the innovator has full control over the supply of the technology when the patent is in force.

A fundamental lesson from economic theory is that monopolies create market distortions. This is typically illustrated comparing a competitive market with a monopoly. In a competitive market, industry rivalry and entry of new firms put pressure on profits and margins and lead to prices that are close to production costs. In the most competitive market environment studied by economists, the perfectly competitive market, profits are equal to zero and the price at which products are sold is equal to the marginal cost of production, that is, the cost of producing an extra unit of product.

When a firm is a monopolist, it faces no direct competition in its industry. In a monopoly market, production is lower and prices are higher than in a competitive market. This occurs because the monopolist has an incentive to create a shortage in the market and sell at high prices to maximize its profits.

The smaller production level and the higher prices that are charged in a monopoly market lead to an overall loss in welfare relative to a perfectly competitive industry. Technically, economists call the difference in surplus between the two market structures the *deadweight loss of monopoly*. This distortion arises because there are consumers in the market willing to pay more than the cost of production for a unit of the good, but they are not served by the monopolist. This occurs because serving these consumers would reduce the profits of the monopolist, as increasing production would reduce market prices and margins. This distortion is not present in a competitive market, where prices equal marginal costs and all customers willing to pay more than the cost of production are served.

The deadweight loss of monopoly is one of the key reasons why countries around the world enact competition policies and establish anti-trust agencies to scrutinize mergers and other industry practices that may harm competition. The reader may then ask the following question: *If monopoly rights generate market distortions, why is it that governments grant patents?*

To answer this question, one needs to remember that an invention is fundamentally new information, which has attributes of what economists call a *public good*. Public goods are nonrival and nonexclusionary in consumption. The use of information by one person does not preclude other people from also using the very same information (nonrivalry). It also means that once a piece of information is disclosed, it is difficult to control its circulation and stop other people from using it (nonexcludability). These attributes of innovation imply that, in the absence of IP rights, a new idea may spread quickly through imitation across markets, substantially reducing the profits of the innovator.

Nobel laureate Kenneth Arrow emphasized another important feature of market transactions involving exchange of information. In information markets, buyers are not willing to pay large sums of money for new information without knowing what they are paying for. At the same time, once buyers know the information they are purchasing, their willingness to pay for it is reduced, because they can exploit what they already know. Joshua Gans and Scott

Stern refer to this property of information as the *paradox of disclosure*: disclosing an innovation increases the buyer's valuation but reduces the inventor's bargaining power. The paradox of disclosure suggests that, in the absence of IP, innovators may be reluctant to share their invention even to firms and users who may find the technology highly valuable.[11]

Innovation is typically the result of research and development (R&D) investments, which in some industries involve very large sums of money. Consider, for example, the case of the pharmaceutical industry where the average R&D expenditures to bring a new drug to market have been estimated to exceed \$1 billion.[12] Without patent protection, competitors would be able to reverse engineer and sell large quantities of pharmaceutical products, driving down market profits to levels close to the production costs. In other words, in the absence of a patent, the innovator would incur all the research cost but would appropriate only limited profits as imitators share the market with the original innovator. This erosion of the innovator's profits can reduce the incentives to develop new technologies. Specifically, firms would have an incentive to *free ride* on research investments of their competitors – that is, to be imitators rather than innovators – and this would lead to lower R&D investments.

The above discussion highlights the key trade-off associated with the patent system. In the absence of patent rights, new products and processes would be available at lower prices, but there would be less innovation because investing in R&D would generate lower returns. Conversely with a patent system in place, consumers will pay higher prices while the patent is in force, but a larger number of new technologies will be developed because returns for R&D investments are higher. A well-designed patent system balances these two aspects. Patent rights promote innovation and increase welfare when the losses in welfare generated by the temporary monopoly distortions are compensated by the gains in welfare created by the development of new products and processes.

## 1.4 The Positive Aspects of Patents

Apart from stimulating innovation investments through the provision of monopoly profits, the patent system has several additional benefits.

The first is the disclosure of the patented technology. The written text and the drawings comprising a patent document provide the details of the product and process innovation protected by the IP. This information is publicly available because patents are published by the patent offices and posted in their free online databases. The disclosed information allows firms and individuals to know who owns the protected technology and to learn about the latest technological developments in their industries. Once the patent expires, the disclosed knowledge enters the public domain and can be freely incorporated in products and processes. Inventors sometimes prefer to avoid the disclosure of information associated with patents and choose instead to protect their technologies through secrecy. In Chapter 5, I will discuss in more detail the strategic choice between patenting and secrecy.

Innovation scholars Alfonso Gambardella, Dietmar Harhoff, and Sadao Nagaoka surveyed inventors to examine the extent to which patent disclosure helps researchers to save time relative to a situation in which the information from patents is not available. On average, inventors report saving about 12 hours of research work, but there is substantial heterogeneity across research areas, with larger impacts in fields such as chemicals and pharmaceuticals.[13]

Second, the patent system is decentralized. Specifically, patents are an economic mechanism in which innovating firms and individuals decide if, when, and how much to invest in R&D. The government provides IP protections to all inventions that satisfy basic patentability requirements. There is no direct involvement of policymakers in directing research investments toward particular technologies, or in deciding the level of R&D investments. This property is particularly beneficial in settings where firms and market agents have more precise information than the government about the technological feasibility and the commercial value of new products. Alternative innovation policy tools, such as inducement prizes or research grants, require greater involvement from policymakers. I will discuss these issues in Chapter 6.

A third benefit of patents is that they reward innovators through market outcomes without the need to use funds raised through general tax revenues. This is especially important when taxation is expected to generate market distortions and for technologies that are not consumed or used by all taxpayers. The strong link with market outcomes also implies that patents provide greater rewards to technologies for which there is larger market demand. This point was highlighted in 1848 by John Stuart Mill in *Principles of Political Economy* where he wrote that

> the reward conferred by it [the patent] depends upon the invention's being found useful, and the greater the usefulness, the greater the reward.[14]

Patents can also be used as assets that can be pledged as collateral to raise debt financing. Finally, patents can provide a powerful market signal on the quality of the underlying technology. This is particularly important for new entrepreneurial ventures for which investors, customers, and suppliers have only limited information. Patents convey information on the novelty of a firm's technology and on its commitment to operate in a specific research area.

A study by Joan Farre-Mensa, Deepak Hegde, and Alexander Ljungqvist confirms this signaling role of patents with a detailed analysis of first-time applications filed at the US patent office. Their research shows that the first patent increases startups' chances of securing funding from venture capitalists over the next three years by 47 percent, of securing a loan by pledging the patent as collateral by 76 percent, and of raising funding from public investors through an IPO by 128 percent. These are large and economically important effects, highlighting the key role that patents play in high-tech entrepreneurship.[15]

## 1.5 The Problems with Patents

In the previous section, I described several positive properties of patent rights identified in the economics literature. Despite these beneficial aspects, a number of scholars and policymakers have raised the concern that patent rights may, in some cases, become a friction that slows down rather than incentivizes innovation investments.

The first issue to consider is that the presence of patent rights requires organizations and individuals interested in accessing the patented technology to engage in *costly transactions* with the patent owners. Negotiating and drafting a licensing contract can be expensive because it often involves the services of specialized lawyers or patent agents. This can be especially taxing for small firms, which tend to be cash constrained.

A second issue that makes patent negotiations challenging is the fact that bargaining often takes place in the presence of *asymmetric information*. Each of the parties involved in a technology transaction may possess some unique knowledge related to the product, the process, or the market in which the innovation is expected to be sold. For example, patentees may have a superior understanding of the patented technology and a more precise assessment of the technological quality of the innovation than the potential licensees. Conversely, licensees who plan to use or sell the patented technology may have a better understanding of the market profitability of the product or process. This asymmetric information may lead to substantial disagreements on the market potential and usefulness of the innovations. Together, transaction costs and incomplete information generate frictions in the market for patents, which may reduce the extent to which technology diffuses. In turn, frictions in the licensing process may lead to a reduction in the incentives to invest in R&D in the first place. Frictions in patent transactions have been shown to be particularly severe in some technology areas of the modern patent landscape where research cycles are quick, where firms have high propensity to patent, and where IP ownership is highly fragmented.[16]

Frictions in patent transactions can be especially problematic in the presence of *cumulative innovation*, that is, when an innovator uses a patented technology to develop a follow-on innovation. This can occur when a new technology is an improvement over an existing technology, or when the development of the new product or process requires the use of a research tool protected by IP. As an example, consider the OncoMouse, a genetically modified mouse developed in 1984 at Harvard University in collaboration with the American chemical company DuPont. This mouse was susceptible to particular types of cancer, and it had the potential to be used as a research tool in medical studies. As a result of its collaboration with Harvard, DuPont obtained rights over the OncoMouse patent. This led many academic researchers to negotiate patent license agreements with DuPont to use the OncoMouse in their research projects during the 1990s.

A study published by Fiona Murray, Philippe Aghion, Mathias Dewatripont, Julian Kolev, and Scott Stern describes how these OncoMouse licensing contracts were often very restrictive. They limited informal mouse exchanges among researchers and granted DuPont shares from future revenues generated by the discoveries obtained using of the genetically modified animal.[17] More crucially, the work by Fiona Murray and her coauthors examines the impact of these strict licensing contracts on academic researchers. They show that patent transactions reduced substantially the propensity of researchers to use the mice and led to lower levels of exploration and diversity in research approaches.[18]

From a theoretical perspective, the effect of patents on cumulative innovation is a complex issue. The literature suggests that anything can happen – patent rights may impede, have no effect on, or even facilitate subsequent technological development. More specifically, the effect that a patent on a base technology has on follow-on innovation depends on the bargaining environment and contracting efficiency between different generations of innovators. Law scholar Edmund Kitch was one of the first to examine this issue. He argued that patents on first-generation technologies can actually facilitate the development of subsequent technologies by enabling the patentee to organize investment in follow-on innovation more efficiently.[19] Economists Jerry Green and Suzanne Scotchmer studied the problem from a bargaining perspective.[20] They argued that patents will not impede follow-on innovation as long as the licensing negotiation between the parties is efficient. Building on the insights of Green and Scotchmer, other studies have shown that patents can block follow-on innovation when bargaining failure occurs. This can arise because of asymmetric information, or because of coordination failures when downstream innovators need to license multiple upstream patents.[21]

Several empirical studies have examined the effect of patents on follow-on innovation. Overall, this literature has shown that most patents do not appear to block cumulative innovation, but there are very specific environments in which they can slow down follow-on research activity.[22]

A final drawback of the patent system is that the profits generated by patents may not provide enough incentives to develop new technologies. This can occur when the market size for a new product or process is small or the ability to pay of consumers is limited. Consider, for example, pharmaceutical research targeting very rare diseases, or diseases predominant in poor countries with low per-capita health spending. The social value of new drugs treating these diseases is large, but the profits that a patentee can obtain may be limited, and this may discourage research investment.[23]

## 1.6 Copyrights

A copyright is the IP protection given to authors of literary, artistic, and musical works. It can also apply to computer programs and movies. The copyright holder has the right to copy, reproduce, publish, or perform the work protected by the IP. Copyrighted works need to be fixed in a *tangible medium of expression*. This means that, to be protected, the creative work needs to be embodied in a digital file or printed or handwritten in a paper document.

In most countries (such as Europe, Japan, and the United States) copyright duration lasts for the life of the author and for seventy years after the death of the author. Historically, Canadian copyright protection lasted for the lifetime of the authors and for fifty years following their death. From December 30, 2022, the term was extended to 70 years after the death of the author. In the United States, work that is created by employees as part of their job is considered "work for hire" and it receives copyright protection for ninety-five years after publication.

Copyright protection is much more limited than patent protection, because it does not protect an idea but only the expression of an idea. This means that if you write an essay about a child playing in the park, copyright prevents other people from copying the very same essay or very similar versions of the essay (e.g., changing a few words, translating it in a different language, or renaming the characters). Other essays about children playing in parks that are not substantially similar to yours will not infringe the copyright.

There is no violation of copyright in the case of *fair use*. This includes educational activities, research, parody, and news reporting. In music, copyright generally does not protect song titles or short phrases. For example, it is not a copyright violation to name a band after someone's else song. American singer Stefani Germanotta is known professionally as Lady Gaga, a name inspired by Queen's song Radio Gaga. Similarly, the rock band Rolling Stones got their name from a blues song recorded by Muddy Waters in 1950.

From a legal perspective, there are two additional important differences to consider when comparing patents and copyrights. The first is that copyright protection does not require examination and screening by a government agency. In fact, copyright protection arises automatically once a work of authorship is fixed in a tangible medium of expression. In most countries, registration to a national agency, such as the US Copyright Office, is a pro-forma administrative act that does not involve substantial screening.[24] In fact, most copyrights are not registered.[25] Registration, which is required to file a lawsuit over ownership or creation, can be made at any time within the life of the copyright.

A second important difference between copyrights and patents is that copyright does not protect against independent invention. Specifically, copyright does not protect against fortuitous similarity arising from independent creation. This implies that in copyright litigation cases, the right holder need not only show that the defendant's work is similar to the one of the plaintiff, but also that the defendant had a reasonable opportunity to view and potentially copy the plaintiff's work.

As in the case of patents, it is difficult to estimate empirically the effect of copyright protection on the creativity of authors. The main challenge is that when a country changes its copyright law, the change affects equally all the authors active in the country. Historical evidence suggests that introduction and strengthening of copyright protection had a large impact on book prices in literature and science.[26] Conversely, estimates obtained from modern data on sales and quality of digital music suggest that reducing the strength of current copyright protection is unlikely to have large effects on the music industry.[27]

Economists Michela Giorcelli and Petra Moser conduct a detailed study of the historical effects of copyright protection on Italian opera using variation in the adoption of copyright laws due to the timing of Napoleon's military victories in Italy. They show that introduction of copyright laws raised both the quantity and quality of nineteenth-century Italian opera.[28]

## 1.7 Other Intellectual Property Rights

Patents and copyrights are the most prevalent forms of IP rights. There are several other types of IP that firms and individual inventors can use to protect knowledge and ideas. Below I briefly discuss some of them, such as trademarks and industrial design.

*Trademarks* are combinations of words, designs, and symbols that are used to identify the products or services of one manufacturer or seller from other goods available on the market. Trademarks can be registered with a national trademark office, and registration provides exclusive rights to use the mark in the country. Unlike patents and copyrights, a trademark does not expire after a set period of time but survives as long as the owner continues to use it and pay renewal fees. In the United States and Canada, trademark registration must be renewed every ten years. Owners of registered trademarks often indicate that their marks have been registered by placing the letter "R" surrounded by a circle (®) next to the relevant word or image.

*Design patents*, or industrial design rights, are IP rights related to the visual characteristics of a product, such as its shape, configuration, or ornaments. For example, the specific shape of a glass bottle, or a furniture decoration, can be protected with design patents. In most countries, the length of industrial design protection is lower than the one from patent protection. In the United States and Canada, these rights expire after about fifteen years.

Other forms of IP rights are also available to inventors. Plant breeder rights (or plant patents) provide rights to inventors who discover or asexually reproduce a new variety of plant. Database rights protect authors of newly assembled databases. Laws introducing database rights were recently enacted in Europe and in the United Kingdom, but this IP right does not currently exist in United States and Canada.

# CHAPTER 2

# Patent Your Idea

*The Patent Office is the mother-in-law of invention.*

– Anonymous

## 2.1 Patent Documents

In Chapter 1, we learned that patents confer upon their owners the right to exclude others from making, using, or selling the patented invention. But what does a patent document look like in practice? In Figure 2.1, I provide an example of the first page of a US patent.

The front page prominently displays the country issuing the patent, which in this example is the United States of America. The patent is identified by a unique patent number, which also features in the front page of the document. In Figure 2.1, this identification code is US 9,976,317 B2. The patent number is the typical way one refers to a specific patent in business contracts or in other legal documents. Sometimes patent attorneys refer to a patent using only the last three digits of the number. In our example, the patent would be referred to as "the '317 patent." The prefix US indicates that this is a patent granted by the United States Patent and Trademark Office (USPTO). The code B2 at the

(12) **United States Patent**
Agha Beigi et al.

(10) Patent No.: **US 9,976,317 B2**
(45) Date of Patent: **May 22, 2018**

(54) **SYSTEM FOR MITIGATING THE EFFECTS OF A SEISMIC EVENT**

(71) Applicant: **THE GOVERNING COUNCIL OF THE UNIVERSITY OF TORONTO,** Toronto (CA)

(72) Inventors: **Hossein Agha Beigi**, Toronto (CA); **Constantin Christopoulos**, Toronto (CA); **Timothy John Sullivan**, Pavia (IT)

(73) Assignee: **THE GOVERNING COUNCIL OF THE UNIVERSITY OF TORONTO,** Toronto (CA)

( * ) Notice: Subject to any disclaimer, the term of this patent is extended or adjusted under 35 U.S.C. 154(b) by 0 days. days.

(21) Appl. No.: **15/100,333**

(22) PCT Filed: **Dec. 2, 2014**

(86) PCT No.: **PCT/CA2014/051154**
§ 371 (c)(1),
(2) Date: **May 30, 2016**

(87) PCT Pub. No.: **WO2015/081431**
PCT Pub. Date: **Jun. 11, 2015**

(65) **Prior Publication Data**
US 2016/0298352 A1     Oct. 13, 2016

**Related U.S. Application Data**

(60) Provisional application No. 61/910,474, filed on Dec. 2, 2013.

(51) **Int. Cl.**
**E04H 9/02**          (2006.01)
**E02D 27/34**         (2006.01)
(Continued)

(52) **U.S. Cl.**
CPC ............. **E04H 9/027** (2013.01); **E02D 27/34** (2013.01); **E04B 1/98** (2013.01); **E04H 9/021** (2013.01);
(Continued)

(58) **Field of Classification Search**
CPC ......... E04H 9/027; E04H 9/025; E04H 9/024; E04H 9/021; E04H 9/028; E04G 23/0218; E02D 27/34; E04B 1/98; E04C 2003/026
See application file for complete search history.

(56) **References Cited**

U.S. PATENT DOCUMENTS

| | | | |
|---|---|---|---|
| 2,053,226 A | * | 9/1936 | Ruge ........................ E04H 9/02 52/113 |
| 3,418,768 A | * | 12/1968 | Cardan .................... E04H 9/02 188/312 |

(Continued)

*Primary Examiner* — Andrew J Triggs
(74) *Attorney, Agent, or Firm* — Elan IP Inc.

(57)          **ABSTRACT**

A building structure having one or more of stories and including at least two columns supporting a first of the stories; where at least one of the columns is supported by at least one brace having a first portion and a second portion. The at least one brace has a first configuration in which the first portion is freely moveable with respect to the second portion such that a gap is formed in the brace preventing the transmission of force axially along the brace, and a second configuration in which the gap is closed by the first portion and the second portion being in contact to permit the transmission of forces axially along the brace. The second configuration occurs when the at least one column undergoes a level of deformation sufficient to force the gap to be closed.

**26 Claims, 29 Drawing Sheets**

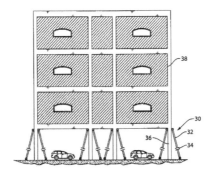

**Figure 2.1.** An example of a patent document

Source: Agha Beigi, H., Christopoulos, C., & Sullivan, T.J. (2018). *System for mitigating the effects of a seismic event* (US Patent No. US 9,976,317 B2). US Patent and Trademark Office. https://image-ppubs.uspto.gov/dirsearch-public/print/downloadPdf/9976317

end provides additional information on the process followed to obtain the patent (e.g., whether there was a pre-grant publication of the document).

The title of the patent gives an idea of the technology being protected. The patent in Figure 2.1 is titled "System for mitigating the effects of a seismic event." The patent lists the inventors who conceived the idea and developed the technology. Often, as in the '317 patent, the innovation is developed by multiple people working within the same organization or in different firms.

Inventors do not necessarily own the patent rights. The actual patent owner is listed in the front page of the document as the assignee. In our example, the assignee is the Governing Council of the University of Toronto. This is a common case, because many firms and organizations have employment contracts that require inventors to automatically transfer patent-rights to their employer.

The document also shows that the USPTO granted the patent in May 2018, but the application to obtain the patent was filed much earlier, in December 2014. This delay between application and grant is due to an extensive examination process that takes place at the patent office. In this chapter, I will provide an overview of the main steps required in the patent application and examination process.

## 2.2  Filing a Patent Application

Most countries have a national patent office where one can file a patent application to obtain intellectual property (IP) protection throughout the territory of the country. In most jurisdictions, patents are granted to the first inventor to file an application, which means that even if a firm or an individual is the first one to discover a new technology, it may not get the patent for it if a competitor files first.

This underscores the importance of keeping new discoveries confidential before a patent application is filed to avoid losing a patent race with competing innovators.

Obtaining a patent involves a long process. According to the 2017 Intellectual Property Indicator Report by the World Intellectual Property Organization (WIPO), it takes on average about 22 months from the moment you file a patent application to the time the patent is granted by the US patent office. In Canada, the average examination process lasts roughly 30 months. At the European patent office, the average examination lasts 23 months, whereas in Japan the process takes less than 16 months.

Before submitting a patent application, an inventor should conduct a preliminary patent search to identify the patents that have already been granted (or applications under review) on related technologies. In the next chapter, I will discuss a variety of online databases that can be used to perform this search. The main goal of the patent search is to determine whether the product or process for which the inventor requests protection has already been patented somewhere in the world. If someone else has already patented the technology (even if in another country), a patent cannot be issued. It is important for innovators to understand the difference between their technologies and those protected by related patents. As we will see below, these related patents will be identified during the examination process and may be used by patent examiners to raise concerns about the novelty of a technology relative to prior art. As I will discuss in the next chapter, understanding the patent landscape in which a firm operates can also be extremely valuable to identify competitors, to spot research trends, and to design a technology strategy.

Patent applications provide a detailed description of the product or process for which IP protection is requested. The description of the technology is typically divided into three parts: the abstract, the specification, and the claims. The abstract gives a short overview of the invention. The guidelines provided by most patent offices suggest that the abstract should be about 50 to 150 words long.

The specification is a comprehensive description of the product or process for which patent protection is demanded. This part of the application also describes related patents and argues how prior art differs from the focal technology in the patent application. The typical legal requirement for the written description of the technology is that it should be sufficiently clear to allow someone with experience in the industry to understand the product and process and potentially be able to reproduce the technology. Often the specification is complemented by visual materials, such as drawings or diagrams.

In writing this part of the application, it is important for inventors to think broadly about their technologies and to consider alternative ways in which their inventions can be made or used. Failure to disclose these alternatives may reduce their ability to use the patent to stop other firms from using similar but not identical versions of the technology.

The claims are the most important part of a patent application. They provide a clear and concise description of the product or process receiving protection. More importantly, the key role of patent claims is to define the boundaries of the invention and the scope of the patent protection. Most patent litigation disputes center around the interpretation of the patent claims, which is crucial to assess whether a patent is valid or infringed.

The University of Toronto's patent illustrated in Figure 2.1 comprises 26 claims. An excerpt from claim 1 and the full claim 2 are reported below.[1]

1   *A building structure having at least one storey comprising: at least one column; at least one brace attached at one end to one side of at least one of said columns and at a second end to a fixed foundation surface; said brace attached to the at least one column at an incline; said at least one*

*brace having a first portion and a second portion; wherein said at least one brace has a first in-use configuration in which the first portion is freely moveable with respect to the second portion such that…*

2 *The building structure according to claim 1, wherein said second portion comprises a tubular shape member and said first portion is sized and otherwise dimensioned to be slidable within the tubular shape member.*

Notice how claims 2 refers to claim 1. In cases like this, we say that claim 1 is an independent claim because it does not refer to any other claim. Conversely, claim 2 is a dependent claim because it specifies and builds on what is described in a previous claim.

Drafting patent claims is not easy because of the technical and legal language required and the importance each word may have in determining the scope of the protection. In some cases, the terms used in the patent claims have specific legal meanings determined through a series of court decisions. Using the wrong term may render the patent invalid or reduce substantially the breadth of the patent. Because of these challenges, it is often recommended that inventors rely on professional patent agents to prepare and file patent applications and to navigate the patent examination process. Patent offices typically provide a list of registered patent agents on their websites. These are individuals who passed a registration examination and are allowed to prepare and file patent applications on behalf of third parties.

## 2.3 Provisional Patent Applications

In the United States, an inventor can begin the patenting process by filing a provisional patent application rather than a regular (non-provisional) application. Provisional patent applications are easy to prepare and relatively inexpensive. A provisional application can be an effective tool to establish a filing date for the patent, and to signal to investors and competitors that the inventor is serious about protecting the innovation.

Provisional applications have a pendency period of one year from the date on which they are filed. The applicant needs to file a non-provisional patent application during the pendency period to benefit from the earlier filing date of the provisional application. The one-year term cannot be extended, and the provisional application cannot be renewed. What makes provisional patent applications easy to draft is that they do not require claims. The applicant has the rights to refer to the invention as "patent pending" during the pendency period.[2]

Filing a US provisional patent application is often recommended to early-stage startup companies as a first step toward developing an IP strategy. This is because provisional patents allow firms to obtain some preliminary patent protection while testing the market and fine-tuning their technologies. The one-year pendency period also allows startup entrepreneurs to raise the funds to cover the expenses related to the non-provisional patent application and its examination process.

## 2.4  Patent Examination and Grant

National patent offices assess whether or not a patent should be granted through a patent examination process. Examination is conducted by patent examiners who have expertise in the technology area of the invention for which protection is requested. Examiners read and analyze the application, identify related prior art and compare it with the technology described in the application, and determine whether the patent should be granted or the application should be rejected.

A number of requirements need to be satisfied in order for an invention to receive patent protection. First, the subject matter must be patentable under the law. What is considered patentable varies across countries, but in general, abstract ideas such as scientific theories, aesthetic creations, and mathematical theorems are not patentable. Often, aspects of nature, such as life forms, are also not patentable, but there are differences across international jurisdictions. For example, the USPTO granted a patent on a genetically modified mouse, but in a case focused on the very same technology, the Supreme Court of Canada ruled that it was not patentable because it was not a *manufacture or composition of matter within the meaning of invention* specified in the Canadian Patent Act.[3]

The second requirement is the novelty of the invention. An invention is considered novel if it possesses some new characteristics. To determine the novelty of an invention, examiners compare the technology with the body of existing knowledge in the technical field available to the public. This body of existing knowledge is called the prior art and encompasses previously issued patents as well as printed scientific publications.[4]

Publication of an invention in scientific journals, its presentation in conferences, or its description in brochures or webpages may jeopardize the patentability of the invention, because it is not possible to obtain a patent if the invention has already been disclosed to the public. Some countries, such as the United States and Canada, provide a one-year grace period during which inventors can disclose their scientific findings before applying for a patent. In Europe, this grace period is not available. This is something important to remember for inventors planning to commercialize their technologies across Europe, because they may benefit from keeping their inventions secret until a European patent application is filed.[5]

The third requirement for patentability is the nonobviousness of the innovation. To satisfy this requirement, the invention needs to differ enough from prior art. To assess whether a technology is nonobvious, the examiners consider whether the development of the new product or process involved an "inventive step" in the sense that someone with ordinary skills in the technology should not find it a trivial modification of the existing available knowledge. Whether an application satisfies the nonobviousness requirement is sometimes hard to predict, because the decision incorporates a certain amount of subjectivity by the examiner.

The final requirement is the utility of the invention, also known as usefulness or industrial applicability. This is typically interpreted as requiring that the technology can be used in an industrial or business setting and that it is not an abstract idea without a clear practical application. Examiners may reject an application for lack of utility if the applicant does not specify any real-world use for the technology. Rejection may also take place when the application makes utility claims that are not credible, for example, if it describes a perpetual-motion machine that breaks the laws of physics.[6]

In their initial assessment of an application, examiners may object to the patentability to one or more of the claims in the application. For example, an examiner may find that one of the claims is too general or that it is too similar to a claim of an existing patent. The concerns of the examiner are summarized in a report called *office action,* that outlines the reasons why the invention fails to meet the patentability standards. An applicant receiving an office action has three options. The first is to respond to the report, trying to convince the examiner that the standard of patentability is met. The second is to accept the report and incorporate the examiner's suggestions in the application, for example, dropping the claims that the examiner deems to be not patentable. The final option is to abandon the application. Typically, the response of the applicant needs to be received within a timeframe specified by the examiner, otherwise the application will be considered abandoned.

Communication with the patent office continues until the examiner allows the application to become a granted patent, the examiner rejects it in a final action, or the inventor decides to abandon the application. Once the application is approved, the inventor receives a notice of allowance, which specifies a fee to be paid to have the patent officially granted.

Numerous recent empirical studies have documented the uncertainty associated with the patent examination process. This line of research has shown that examiners differ substantially in their propensity to grant patents, even within a narrow technology area. This implies that the strictness of the review process faced by an application will depend on the examiner assigned to the file.[7]

## 2.5 Publication of Patent Applications

Most patent offices publish the patent applications they receive in publicly available online databases eighteen months after their filing date. The public disclosure of this information has important strategic effects, because it implies that inventors can hide their decision to request a patent, and the details of the invention, only for a limited period of time. After eighteen months, this information will be available to market competitors and to other firms and individuals interested in the technology.

Historically, US patents applications were kept secret, and competitors learned about a new patent only when it was granted. This changed in 1999 when the US Congress passed a legislation that harmonized the US system with the majority of international patent offices and required publication eighteen months after filing. This legislation attracted substantial opposition. In a letter to Congress, twenty-six Nobel laureates warned that the change *will prove very damaging to American small inventors and thereby discourage the flow of new inventions that have contributed so much to America's superior performance.*[8] The concern was that large firms could use the early information disclosed in patent applications of small firms to compete more aggressively in the product and technology markets against these smaller players. To assess the empirical validity of this concern, several empirical studies have estimated the effects of the policy on firms' innovation incentives. Overall, these studies suggest that the benefits of transparency outweigh its costs.

One of the most important benefits of the publication of patent applications is that it facilitates licensing contracts, which in turn allow patentees to obtain royalty revenue before a patent is granted. The basic idea is that the publication provides verifiable information that an innovator can use to sue other firms for infringement and to demand royalties for the period between the publication date and the patent grant date. These benefits may be particularly salient for individuals and small firms, which often rely on other industry players for the commercialization of the technologies they develop.

Consistent with this idea, a study by Deepak Hegde and Hong Luo finds that US patent applications are significantly more likely to be licensed 18 months after their filing date, that is, once the information is published.[9] Of course, some uncertainty remains even after the publication of a patent application, because the outcome of the examination may not be successful, and the application may be rejected. In other words, if a licensing contract takes place before a patent is granted, the contract will typically include a provision that contemplates the case of rejection of the patent application. At the end of the examination process, if the patent is officially granted, the uncertainty on the IP protection is reduced even more. As in the case of the disclosure of patent applications, this second drop in uncertainty associated with patent grants also has beneficial effects on the market for technology. This has been documented empirically in a study by Joshua Gans, David Hsu, and Scott Stern, who show a substantial increase in the probability that a patent is licensed once its status changes from pending to granted.[10]

## 2.6  International Patent Protection

National patents grant IP rights only within the boundaries of the country issuing them. In other words, an American patent can be used to block others from practicing the technology in the United States, but it cannot stop someone from copying the technology in Canada or in Japan. To obtain protection in a foreign country, an innovator needs to obtain the relevant foreign patent.

There are two main channels through which one can obtain a foreign patent. The first is by filing an application in the patent office of the foreign country. The second approach is to apply for the foreign patent at the national patent office under the Patent Cooperation Treaty (PCT). The PCT route allows an applicant to seek international patent protection, selecting among more than 150 countries.

Despite the centralized nature of the PCT filing system, each national patent office reviews the application and issues the patent according to its national laws. This means that the very same PCT application can lead to a patent in one country and be rejected in another, because each national patent office follows its own standards for novelty, utility, and nonobviousness. Moreover, as I discussed above, other aspects of patent laws, such as the patentability of a subject matter, also differ across countries.

Obtaining international patent protection through the PCT is often more expensive and takes longer than filing for a unique national patent. PCT is the common route for large multinational corporations that sell worldwide, and it is not frequently used by startup ventures, which often do not have the financial resources to obtain a wide international protection. The IP strategy commonly used by startup entrepreneurs that intend to sell only in a small number of countries is to file national applications directly at the relevant national patent offices.

There has been a substantial increase in PCT applications in the past decade. According to the WIPO, in 2020, there were 275,900 PCT applications. China was the largest user of the PCT, with 68,720 applications, followed by the United States. Japan ranks third, followed by South Korea and Germany.[11]

Technology managers typically consider various issues when they decide in which countries to apply for a patent. The first one is the size of the market in the country. It may not be worthwhile to apply for a patent in a country if local demand for the technology is limited and the number of consumers willing to buy the product is low, or the price that they are willing to pay is modest. Second, one considers the presence of potential competitors and licensees in the country. In the absence of a foreign patent, international competitors may freely use and copy the technology in the foreign country. This may have important effects on firms' competitive advantage and industry competition. It is also important to assess whether potential licensees are operating in a country. A firm may not have the resources or capabilities required to directly operate in a foreign country, but the presence of a pool of potential licensees may allow the firm to extract profits through royalties and licensing fees.

Finally, managers need to consider how strong patent protection is in the foreign country. This is because the profitability of a foreign patent depends on how costly it is to enforce it in the case of infringement. This point has been documented by several studies in the innovation literature.

Mercedes Delgado, Margaret Kyle, and Anita McGahan have examined the impact of TRIPS (trade-related aspects of intellectual property rights), a component of the World Trade Organization agreement enacted in 1995 to facilitate international trade. TRIPS required member countries to implement patent protection for knowledge-intensive products, such as biopharmaceuticals, computers, and telecommunications. This led to big policy changes in several developing and least developed countries that did not have strong patent rights at the time. Their analysis shows that international trade in knowledge-intensive products increased substantially after TRIPS implementation. In particular, after strengthening their IP laws, developing countries were able to import more technologies from high-income countries, especially in the patent-intensive information and communications technology sector.[12]

A study by Iain Cockburn, Jean Lanjouw, and Mark Schankerman examines the international diffusion of pharmaceutical products and shows that the patent policies adopted by governments strongly affect how quickly new drugs are launched in their countries. The study shows that longer, stronger patent protection powerfully accelerates diffusion of new drugs, and that foreign firms tend to avoid countries with weak systems of IP rights.[13]

## 2.7 Patent Duration and Maintenance Fees

In Chapter 1, I discussed how patent systems provide temporary monopoly rights to incentivize innovation investments. Patent protection does not last forever, and the technical knowledge can be freely used by the public once the patent expires. In most countries, patents have a duration of twenty years from the filing date of the patent application.

During the twenty-year patent term, patentees are required to pay patent maintenance fees (sometime also called renewal fees) to the patent office. Failure to pay these fees leads to the expiration of the patent right before the maximum duration. The amount and the frequency of payments varies across patent offices. In the United States, maintenance fees are due three times during the lifetime of the patent: at 3.5, 7.5, and 11.5 years after the date of the grant. In Canada, they are due each year.

In most countries, maintenance fees tend to increase over the life of the patent. For example, in 2020 the required payments at the USPTO were $1,600 at 3.5 years, $3,600 at 7.5 years, and $7,400 at 11.5 years. This monotonic increase of the fees has the advantage of removing monopoly deadweight losses for technologies that generate little profits. A study by innovation economist Carlos Serrano finds that about 50 percent of US patents held by large companies expire before the last renewal fee, and the fraction is higher (between 60–77 percent) for smaller firms and individual inventors. This implies that, for many technologies, monopoly distortions do not last for twenty years and that many technologies reach the public domain after a much shorter period of time.[14]

In practice, most patent offices use patent maintenance fees as a tool to finance their activities, and there is no reason to believe that the current level of fees provides an optimal balance between monopoly distortions and innovation incentives. How to optimally structure patent fees and adjust other patent policy instruments (such as application fees, maximum duration, and patentability standards) is an active line of research in theoretical industrial organization.[15]

In most countries, renewal fees are lower for smaller firms (typically defined as those with less than 50 employees) and for individual inventors. Historically, patent fees have varied substantially over time and across countries.[16]

## 2.8 Protecting Software: Patents vs. Copyright

In principle, software can be protected using two types of IP: patents and copyrights. Choosing between these two forms of protection is not easy, and it is not uncommon for startups to struggle when they face this strategic decision. I have witnessed these challenges several times in my meetings with ventures of the Creative Destruction

Lab, Canada's leading program for software entrepreneurs working on AI, blockchain, and quantum technologies.

The issue is difficult for several reasons. The first is that the legal status of software patents is uncertain. This is particularly the case in the United States, where patentability of software has evolved substantially over time and there is still some uncertainty about which software inventions can be patented. A series of important judicial decisions shaped software patentability standards from the 1970s to current days. A landmark Supreme Court decision in 1972 (*Gottschalk v. Benson*) held that software could not be patented and that the suitable protection for a computer code was copyright. The view of the court changed in 1981 (*Diamond v. Diehr*) when it examined a patent involving a computer connected to a machine that cured rubber. The court held that patenting of software tied to physical or mechanical processes was possible.

This new view on software patentability led to a growth in software patenting during the 1980s and 1990s as computers and IT became a crucial component of the US economy. Patentability of software expanded even more in 1998 when a decision of the Court of Appeal for the Federal Circuit (*State Street Bank and Trust v. Signature Financial Corporation*) stated that mathematical algorithms were patentable as long as they were not "disembodied," that is, lacking a useful application.[17]

The courts' view on software patentability changed in more recent years, especially with the 2014 Supreme Court ruling (*Alice v. CLS Bank*) claiming that software patents that were simply implementing an abstract idea on a generic computer were not valid. This decision was followed by many lower court rulings rejecting software patents for being too abstract.

Overall, the history of software patentability indicates that the uncertainty faced by software firms is greater than the one faced by firms operating in other technology fields. There is not only uncertainty on whether a software patent application will be granted by the patent office, but also on the ability of firms to enforce a granted patent, as the views of the courts change over time.

The alternative IP protection to a software patent is copyright. Copyright protection can be obtained quickly, with no uncertainty, and at little cost. In this respect, copyright has advantages over patents, which involve long examination periods and significant expenses related to filing and maintenance.

At the same time, copyright protection is much narrower than what is offered by a patent. The key difference between the two forms of IP is that copyright protects the code itself (the expression of the idea) but not the invention that leads to a solution of a problem (the idea). This implies that copyright can be used to block someone from duplicating a software program or from copying a portion of the code, but it cannot stop someone from using an alternative way to code the solution, even if the underlying general idea behind the two codes appears similar.

# CHAPTER 3

# Patent Analytics

*In God we trust. All others must bring data.*

– Edwards Deming[1]

## 3.1 Patents and Data-Driven Decision Making

Designing and implementing an effective technology strategy requires a good understanding of the technology field in which a firm operates, its key players, their competitive advantage, and new innovation trends. The best way to reach this understanding is to collect and analyze data on the development and commercialization of new technologies. As implied by this chapter's epigraph quotation of Edwards Deming, managers should not rely only on their intuition when data are available.

Patents granted by patent offices around the world are a natural source of data for this type of analysis. In the words of Professor Zvi Griliches:

> patent statistics loom up as a mirage of wonderful plentitude and objectivity. They are available; they are by definition related to inventiveness, and they are based on what appears to be an objective and only slowly changing standard.[2]

Patent data are widely available. In many countries and geographical regions, such as the United States, Canada, Europe, and Japan, large datasets can be accessed through the patent office websites for bulk download at low cost or for free. Patent data provide very detailed information, including a description of the technology, the identity of the firm owning the patent, the inventors involved in developing the innovation, and a list of related patent documents (the patent citations). This makes them a very attractive data source for the statistical analysis and the measurement of innovation activity in a technology field. In this chapter, I discuss a variety of patent analytics methods and measures that can be used to perform this type of study.

The innovation literature has shown that technologies with greater impact on social welfare and economic growth are more likely to be patented.[3] Despite this finding, one qualification should be kept in mind. Not all inventions are patented, which implies that patent data may in some cases miss important aspects of the technology landscape. This may be especially the case in industries where trade secrecy is a common technology strategy. I will discuss trade secrecy more in detail in Chapter 4.

## 3.2 Data Sources

On the websites of most national patent offices, one can find search engines that allow one to search for the full text of patents granted and for published patent applications. These portals allow users to perform various types of searches. For example, in the USPTO portal, one can enter keywords capturing some specific technology (e.g., "telephone," or "clarinet," or "fridge") and obtain the list of patents for which these terms appears in the title or in the abstract. Alternatively, one can enter the name of a firm and obtain all the patents assigned to (owned by) the firm.

Clicking on each of the patents listed in the search result, it is possible to obtain the full text of the document, which includes information on the names of the inventors, the assignee of patent, the technological classification, the filing date, and the grant date. The website of the USPTO also provides basic aggregate statistics about US patenting activity across technology areas.

These types of search portals are available through most national patent offices and the World Intellectual Property Organization (WIPO). The Organisation for Economic Co-operation and Development (OECD) also provides a variety of statistical indicators on international patenting activity.

The website https://patentsview.org hosts a comprehensive patent data platform, PatentsView, which is managed by the Office of the Chief Economist at the USPTO. PatentsView allows for bulk data download in various formats. The downloadable files encompass several datasets covering the past forty years of US patent data. The data available on this platform are extremely detailed and complete. For example, one can download the full text of all patent claims (including dependency and sequence) for all US patents granted from 1976 to present. The resulting dataset is a spreadsheet with more than 100,000,000 rows and a size of roughly 40 GB. Such big datasets are typically used by researchers examining innovation activity spanning multiple years and numerous sectors of the US economy.

For many technology strategy decisions, one does not need such large datasets. In many cases, the technology landscape that has to be considered by a decision maker can be well captured by a sample of few hundred patents or even a few dozen patents. In these cases, a useful data source is Google Patent Search™ service, which will be referred to for the rest of the book as "Google Patents."[4] This is a specialized search engine that allows one to perform international patent searches and download an Excel file with the relevant search results. The platform can be accessed at https://patents.google.com.

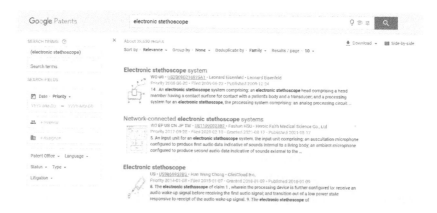

**Figure 3.1.** Google Patent Search™ service
Source: Google and the Google logo are trademarks of Google LLC.

Figure 3.1 provides an example of the outcome of a Google Patents search. The terms "electronic stethoscope" were entered in the search box. The search output is a list of patents that are related to the technology in the query.

The search fields available in the portal allow one to narrow the search, focusing on specific national patent offices (e.g., only US patents), precise time windows (e.g., only patents granted between 2014 and 2017), or particular assignees and inventors. The results from a search can be downloaded in Excel format and analyzed with standard statistical packages.

In the remainder of this chapter, I will discuss how a sample of patents can provide a large amount of information that can be very useful for strategic decision making. Managers can use patent data to construct several measures and indexes that describe the business environment and the technological landscape in which a firm operates or plans to operate. In the Appendix of the book, I present a simple patent analytics report, which applies some of the key concepts described in the chapter.

## 3.3 Tracking Firms' Innovation

One of the most common uses of patent analytics relates to the collection and analysis of data on the patenting of a firm's closest competitors. In Google Patents, one can perform this analysis by searching for patents assigned to specific firms. For instance, by typing:

assignee: (Blackberry Limited)

in the Google Patents search box, one obtains the list of patents for Blackberry, one of the top Canadian patentees. One can narrow the search to the most recent patents of the company and even identify patent applications that have not yet been granted by the patent office. Similar searches can be conducted in the portals of leading patent offices, as well as in PatentsView.

Analysis of newly issued patents can help managers to infer what future products a competitor will sell. Patent data can even allow speculation about possible changes in the business model of a company. Take, for example, US patent 8,615,473 obtained by Amazon in December 2013 titled *"Method and system for anticipatory package shipping."* The technology in this patent led economists Ajay Agrawal, Joshua Gans, and Avi Goldfarb to conjecture that Amazon's business model may change in the coming years, shifting from a "shopping-then-shipping" approach to a "shipping-then-shopping" strategy. In this alternative business model, Amazon would ship customers the products that it predicts they would buy rather than waiting customers to order them online.[5]

Patent searches are an easy and inexpensive source of data that permit tracking of new technological developments of specific companies. Patents are a leading indicator of firms' business activities, in the sense that a firm filing multiple patents in a technology area is likely to sell new products in that space. In this respect, patent data may help managers understand whether their competitors are exploring new product lines, exiting from particular technology areas, or substantially increasing their research activity on specific aspects of their products.

Searching for the name of competing firms is useful when one expects most new technologies to be developed by established firms of known identity. A limitation of this approach is that it may miss new competitors of which a manager is unaware. These can be newly established companies or existing firms that diversify into new technology areas. In the next section, I discuss ways to address this problem by performing searches related to keywords associated to a specific invention.

Even when someone knows the name of the firm for which patent data need to be retrieved, it is important to take into account that measurement error can affect the search. For example, large firms may file applications using different names (e.g., IBM or International Business Machine) that are not always standardized by the search portal. Missing one of these names may give an incomplete sample of patents.

For searches related to smaller firms, a common problem is that one may have to distinguish between several companies with the same name. Consider, for example, a manager who needs to identify patents by a small firm from San Francisco called "Tech Systems Inc." that develops air conditioning systems. A patent search may yield a large number of documents, but this is probably because there are many firms named Tech Systems Inc. in the patent data. In cases like this, managers can use the geographical information in the patents (focus only on patents by firms called Tech Systems Inc. based in San Francisco) or information on the specific technology area (focus on heating, ventilation, and air conditioning patents) to obtain a more accurate sample.

## 3.4 Identifying Innovation Trends

Each patent is classified by the patent office using a detailed system of classes and subclasses. Most countries around the world use the Cooperative Patent Classification (CPC) scheme, a system jointly developed by several international patent offices. Classes typically demarcate broad technological areas, whereas subclasses delineate more detailed technical fields within the scope of a class. The classification scheme is hierarchical; higher-level, broader classes are subdivided in lower-level, finer subclasses. For example, technologies related to dumbbell gym equipment are often allocated to CPC subclass A63B 21/072. One can find this subclass within the following groupings:

*A Human Necessities*
*A63 Sports; Games; Amusements*
*A63B Apparatus for Physical Training, Gymnastics, Swimming, Climbing, or Fencing, Ball Games, Training Equipment*
*A63B21 Exercising Apparatus for Developing or Strengthening the Muscles or Joints of the Body by Working Against a Counterforce, with or without Measuring Devices*
*A63B 21/072 Dumb-bells, Bar-bells or the like*

Plotting the patenting activity in a class (or in a group of classes) over time can be a useful way to examine whether there have been changes in technology trends. A substantial acceleration in the patenting activity registered in a class may suggest that the technology area is attracting a lot of new R&D investments. Conversely, sharp declines in patenting activity may suggest a shift away from the technology field.

To construct figures describing timing trends of patenting, one can use the dates when patents are granted or the dates when patents are filed. Filing dates are often preferable, because they are

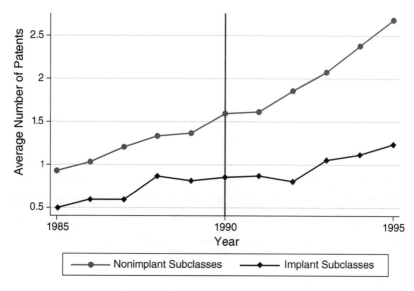

**Figure 3.2.** Patenting trends in two groups of subclasses
Source: Galasso, A., & Luo, H. (2022). When does product liability risk chill innovation? Evidence from medical implants. *American Economic Journal: Economic Policy, 14*(2), 366–401, Figure 1. https://doi.org/10.1257/pol.20190757

closer to when the technologies were discovered and may serve as better proxy for the time of invention.

As an example, the red line in Figure 3.2 (from a study I conducted with Hong Luo) plots the patenting activity in patent subclasses related to medical implant technologies. These are medical devices or tissues that are placed inside or on the surface of the body, such as pacemakers or silicone breast implants. The blue line in the same figure shows patenting in other medical devices patent subclasses, such as stethoscopes or syringes. Each patent is dated using the year in which its application was filed.[6]

In the late 1980s, a series of unexpected and widespread problems arose with some medical implants, which lead to a dramatic surge in medical liability litigation around 1990. The goal of the study that

I conducted with Hong Luo was to examine whether this surge in liability litigation had an impact on medical implant innovation. One may expect product liability risk to chill innovation investments, which in turn may slow down technological progress in the area. The figure supports to this idea. It shows that patenting in the two technologies evolved in parallel up to 1990, but then patenting in medical implants slowed down relative to non-implant medical technologies after 1990. In other words, the two technology areas followed similar trends before 1990 but diverged after 1990. In Chapter 8, I will discuss in greater depth the link between innovation, health, and safety risk.

## 3.5 Examining the Geographic Distribution of Innovation Activity

Each patent reports information on the locations of the inventors and the assignees. One can use this information to examine the geographical aspects of the patenting activity in a technology area. For example, location data can be used to assess whether patenting is concentrated in a few specific regions, or whether it is mostly driven by national or by foreign innovators. As I will discuss in Chapter 7, this data can speak to the quality and specialization of the R&D workforce located in a region, and thus inform firms' location strategies.

A striking feature of economic geography is the large variation in productivity across regions. Research by economist Enrico Moretti documents that after adjusting for skill composition, average wages in the highest- and lowest-paying US metropolitan areas differ by approximately a factor of three. Such dispersion is also evident when one compares patenting activity across regions. Silicon Valley and Boston are popular examples of outlier regions, significantly more productive than others in terms of innovation.[7]

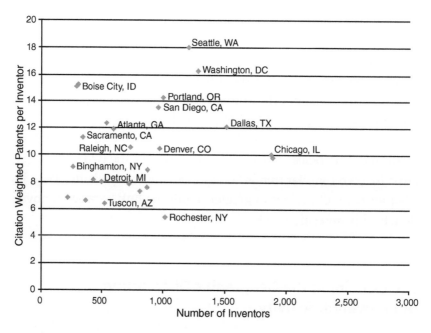

**Figure 3.3.** Variation in regional innovation – computers and communication patenting in 1995
Source: This figure was previously published in Agrawal, A., Cockburn, I., Galasso, A., & Oettl, A. (2014). Why are some regions more innovative than others? The role of small firms in the presence of large labs. *Journal of Urban Economics, 81,* 149–165, Figure 1. https://doi.org/10.1016/j.jue.2014.03.003. Copyright 2014 Elsevier/ScienceDirect.

Figure 3.3 (from research that I conducted with Ajay Agrawal, Iain Cockburn, and Alexander Oettl) illustrates such variation using US patent data on computers and communication technologies. Specifically, the graph was constructed collecting data on patents filed in 1995 across a variety of classes related to communication, computer hardware and software, computer peripherals, and information storage. Patents were allocated to cities based on the location of the inventors.[8]

Strikingly, the figure shows that even cities of similar size in terms of the number of local inventors often differ substantially in terms of their innovation productivity (number of patented inventions per inventor). Take, for example, Rochester, NY, and Portland, OR. The two cities had a similar number of innovators working in the computer and communications industry in 1995, but inventors in Portland generated almost twice the number of patents.[9]

## 3.6 Identify the Most Innovative Research Employees of a Firm

Another possible use of patent data involves exploiting the names of the inventors listed in a patent to study the research productivity and the structure of research teams active in a firm. Once the patents granted to a firm have been identified, one can look at the names of the inventors on the patents and examine their specialization and productivity.

Using the inventors' names, one can also try to infer the organization of the R&D laboratories of the firm. For example, assume that you observe that inventors A, B, and C always appear together on patents related to technology X, and inventors D, E, and F always appear together on patents related to technology Y. From this information, one can infer that the firm has two separate research units: one for technology X, employing inventors A, B and C, and one for technology Y, employing inventors D, E, and F.

One can even go a step further and use the locations of the inventors to infer where the R&D labs are located. For instance, inventors A, B, and C may be located in California and inventors D, E, and F in Massachusetts, suggesting that the research unit for technology X is based in California and the one for technology Y is based in Massachusetts.

Economists have used patent data to address several research questions related to the behavior of inventors. For example, Ufuk Akcigit, Salomé Baslandze, and Stefanie Stantcheva show that superstar inventors (those in the top 1 percent of quality-adjusted patenting) are significantly affected by top tax rates when deciding where to locate. This is especially the case for foreign-born inventors and those working in multinational companies.[10]

## 3.7  Empirical Analysis of Patent Citations

When filing a patent application, inventors are required to disclose known prior art that is related to the technology for which the patent is requested. These references are called patent citations and resemble the bibliographical references of academic articles or books. Despite their similarity to references in academic studies, patent citations differ from academic references in some important ways. First, while the references in research articles are chosen by the authors, patent citations may also be added to the document by patent examiners during the examination process. Second, academic articles may be cited for a variety of reasons, and it is not uncommon for authors to refer to literature that is only marginally related to their research to suggest that their work has a broad and multidisciplinary impact. Conversely, patent applicants have strong incentives not to cite unnecessary prior patents because this may jeopardize their claims of novelty.[11]

Patent search portals, such as Google Patents, often include information on the citations made by each patent document and the citations received (i.e., the list of other patent documents that refer to the focal patent). Citation data are used in the patent analytics literature for two main purposes: (i) as a measure of patent value and (ii) as a measure of knowledge flows.

Once you have identified all the patents owned by a firm, a natural question to ask is: which of these patents is the most important? As with many other business assets, it is usual to expect a lot of variance in the value generated by the patents owned by a firm. This implies that simply counting the patents of a firm may not be a very informative measure of its innovative output.[12]

Consider two firms: firm A and firm B. Assume that both firms have 10 patents each. Let us take the case in which the patents of firm A are much more valuable than those of firm B. For example, they were licensed more widely, are related to more profitable products and, overall, have larger impact on the industry. How can this be noticed in the patent data?

A standard approach used to capture such asymmetries in patent value is to look at the number of *citations received* by the patent. The idea is that when a patent document receives a lot of citations from subsequent patent applications, this reveals that the patent had an important impact on subsequent research in the technology field.[13]

A study by Bronwyn Hall, Adam Jaffe, and Manuel Trajtenberg supports this metric looking at the impact of receiving patent citations on the market value of publicly traded firms. They find that, on average, an extra citation per patent boosts firms' stock market value by 3 percent. This average effect appears to be predominantly driven by the most highly cited patents: firms having two to three times the median number of citations per patent display a 35 percent value premium compared to the other firms in the study. [14]

Very often, new technologies developed by one firm affect innovation activities of other firms. This happens, for example, when an innovation developed by firm A is licensed and used by firm B, and then improved by firm B. But the technical knowledge developed by a firm may reach other firms even in the absence of licensing. For example, scientists of firm A may leave the company to go to work for firm B and exploit some of the knowledge they generated in firm A when working on their new research projects at firm B. More generally, managers of firm B may read the patents of firm A, or reverse engineer its products, and use this information to develop new products that are different than those developed by firm A but that somehow extend or build on some of firm A's innovations.

When the technology of firm A spills outside its boundaries, economists say that there are *knowledge flows* from one firm to another, or they say that firm A has generated *knowledge spillovers*. Identifying knowledge spillovers may be very valuable for managers. Knowledge flows provide information on how connected the technologies of different firms are, on whether the research of a firm has a big impact on the industry, or on whether two firms rely on each other in their research projects.

Identifying knowledge flows was considered an empirical challenge for many years. Nobel laureate Paul Krugman wrote in 1991:

> *knowledge flows are invisible; they leave no paper trail by which they may be measured and tracked, and there is nothing to prevent the theorist from assuming anything about them that she likes.*[15]

An important research breakthrough took place in 1993 when Adam Jaffe, Manuel Trajtenberg, and Rebecca Henderson realized that knowledge flows do sometimes leave a paper trail in the form of citations in patents. The idea of these three scholars was that it is possible to use the citation patterns observed in patents to measure the extent of knowledge spillovers across firms.[16]

Intuitively, consider examining the patents granted to two firms, firm A and firm B. Reading these patent documents, you may notice that the patents of firm B cite the patents of firm A much more often than the patents of firm A cite the patents of firm B. This suggests that firm B relies on firm A's knowledge much more heavily than firm A relies on firm B's knowledge. In other words, relative differences in citation frequencies suggest that firm A's knowledge spills over and affects firm B's research. This insight opened up a large literature that exploited citation patterns as a proxy for knowledge flows and empirically examined the determinants of research spillovers.

While this research area has mostly exploited the citations reported in the front page of the patent documents, recent work by Kevin Bryan, Yasin Ozcan, and Bhaven Sampat has shown that the bibliographical references reported in the specification text of the patents can also be very informative. Specifically, they show that in-text citations to academic research in a firm's patents are strongly correlated with the firm's reliance on public sector research and open science.[17]

## 3.8 Litigation, Licensing, and Patent Examiners' Data

A leading source of information on US patent litigation cases is the Public Access to Court Electronic Records (PACER) system. This dataset provides comprehensive information on litigated cases recorded electronically by US courts beginning from the 2000s. PACER charges a per-page downloading fee, which makes it expensive to download a large number of records. Several private companies in the United States and internationally sell large datasets on patent litigation activity. A survey by law scholars David Schwartz and Ted Sichelman provides a comprehensive overview of these sources of data.[18]

The full text of US judicial decisions related to patents cases may be downloaded from several law portals, such as LexisNexis Quick Law. North American universities often subscribe to these databases and give access to their students. Decision documents contain a detailed description of the litigated dispute, the judicial decision, and the jurisprudence used to reach decisions.

In the United States, data on patent licensing and cross-licensing is often limited to the contracts that are disclosed to the Securities and Exchange Commission (SEC) by publicly traded companies. Typically, firms disclose in these filings only licensing deals that qualify as material transactions under the securities laws. These security files are available on the Electronic Data Gathering, Analysis and Retrieval (EDGAR) database of the SEC, as well as on other data platforms such as Lexis and Westlaw. Unfortunately, publicly disclosed licenses represent only the tip of the iceberg, and many licensing contracts are kept confidential because they do not represent material transactions or do not involve publicly traded firms. Some private companies sell datasets that combine the licensing information in EDGAR with other license deals available from other sources.

The data available from the USPTO also provides information on the patent examiners involved in the screening process for each patent application. These data have been used in empirical work to assess the differences in leniency across patent examiners.

# CHAPTER 4

# Patent Litigation and Licensing

*The life of a patent solicitor has always been a hard one.*

– Judge Giles Rich[1]

## 4.1 An Introduction to Patent Litigation

A patent is *infringed* when someone makes, uses, or sells the patented technology without the permission of the patentee. Patent owners who believe their patent is infringed can sue the alleged infringer for damages.

In most countries, patentees have the right to sue infringers only after their patents are granted. Nonetheless, they can also obtain "reasonable compensation" related to infringement occurring between the date on which the application was made public (typically 18 months after filing) and the date the patent was granted.

Defendants often respond to infringement suits arguing that infringement did not occur. Frequently, they also countersue for *invalidity*, claiming that the patent should not have been granted by the patent office. Patent invalidation can take place if, for example, the court finds that the invention lacks novelty over some prior art, or that the patented invention was obvious to someone skilled in the technology area. In the case of successful invalidation, the technology becomes freely available. Notice that this is beneficial not only for the firm that challenged the patent but also for other firms interested in using the technology. This positive effect that invalidation may have on other industry players (competitors in particular) implies that, in some cases, firms may have only limited incentives to challenge the validity of patents.[2]

If a court finds that the patent is infringed, it typically grants an *injunction*, which is an order to stop the infringing activity. In addition, the court may award monetary *damages* for losses suffered by the patentee as a result of the infringement. There are two leading doctrines on how patent damages should be determined. The first one, "unjust enrichment," is focused on punishing the infringer, which is required to give up all the profits from infringement. The second doctrine, "lost profits," instead focuses on compensating patent holders and maintaining their incentives to invest in R&D. The prevailing rule in the United States is lost profits.[3]

Many leading patent litigation cases take place in the United States because this is a very important market for many multinational firms. The American court system has three levels. Initially the case is filed in one of the regional district courts. Parties can appeal the district court ruling to the Court of Appeals for the Federal Circuit (CAFC). Losing appeal parties may seek a review of the decision at the Supreme Court.

US patent law allowed patent owners substantial flexibility in which venue to choose when suing for infringement. This led many patentees to engage in "forum-shopping," with firms choosing courts perceived to be friendly to patent owners, or courts more likely to award large jury verdicts or to set early trial dates. A 2017 Supreme Court decision, *TC Heartland v. Kraft Foods Group Brands*, reduced substantially the ability of patentees to pick their preferred venue. In this ruling, the Supreme Court stated that the proper venue for a patent case is where the defendant firm is incorporated or where the defendant has committed acts of infringement and has a regular and established place of business.

Douglas Kline describes patent litigation as the "sport of kings" because of its high costs, its complexity, and its rare nature. This metaphor is supported by the estimates provided by innovation and law scholars James Bessen and Michael Meurer. According to their computations, the legal fees required to enforce a patent in a US infringement case with damages below $1 million are about $500,000. For suits with $1–$25 million at risk, the estimated cost is $2 million, and for suits with damages above $25 million is about $4 million.[4] These are very large expenditures, especially for individual inventors and startups that are often cash constrained.

The challenges faced by small players trying to enforce their patents against large incumbent firms are exemplified by the story of Robert Kearns, the inventor of the intermittent windshield wiper. Kearns had several patents on a new windshield wiper that moved at intervals rather than in a constant back and forth motion. In 1962, he mounted the technology on his car and drove it to Ford's headquarters. Despite an initial interest in the technology, Ford executives decided not to license the patents from Kearns. In 1969, Ford released the first car with intermittent windshield wipers in the United States, followed by Mercedes-Benz and several other major car manufacturers. In many of these models, the technologies were quite similar to those patented by Kearns. As a response, Kearns filed lawsuits against 26 car manufacturers to obtain patent infringement damages. Enforcing his patents against these big players was very challenging, and the resulting legal battle was long and painful. It took Kearns more than a decade to receive some form of compensation from Ford and Chrysler.[5]

Patent litigation is a rare event. Bessen and Maurer document how suits are initiated for only a small fraction of patents (about 2 percent). Moreover, the vast majority (about 96 percent) of patent suits are settled before the judicial decision.

Even if the chances of getting involved in a patent litigation are very small, this does not imply that litigation risk should not be taken seriously by innovators and technology users. As discussed above, the monetary costs in terms of legal fees and damages can be extremely large in IP litigation cases. Moreover, firms involved in patent litigation may experience additional non-monetary costs related to diverting their attention from technological development to a legal battle. The uncertainty associated with the litigation process may also induce firms to pause or terminate research programs until there is more clarity over the patent landscape. Finally, even if litigation does not take place, the threat of litigation can have important effects on licensing negotiations and on the decision to enter a particular technology area.

A study by Deepak Somaya shows that patent suits are less likely to be settled when the patentee has strong strategic stakes in the litigated patent and the underlying technology. When the product or the process protected by the patent are crucial for the competitive advantage of the firm, and access by rivals dramatically reduces firm's profitability, the patentee has strong incentive to block the alleged infringer by enforcing the patent.[6]

Research by Jean Lanjouw and Mark Schankerman shows that patents of small firms are more likely to be litigated than those of larger companies.[7] This empirical regularity is consistent with one of the key predictions from game theory: repeated interaction facilitates cooperation. A fundamental result in game theory, known as the "folk theorem," is that in strategic situations where cooperation is hard to achieve, players may end up cooperating if they are patient enough and interact frequently with each other. Consider the following hypothetical situation. You are a manager of firm A and you think that firm B is infringing one of your patents. You may prefer not to litigate with firm B if you are also likely to potentially infringe firm B's patents in the future. In other words, you may be better off avoiding the litigation of the current patent infringement if this makes it more likely that you will not be sued in the future. More broadly, repeated interaction allows large firms to settle patent disputes more easily by using their large patent portfolios to trade intellectual property. This is not feasible if firms are small, because they may not have enough technologies to trade, or because they may be perceived as unlikely to be present in the future.

As suggested by Judge Giles Rich in the epigraph of this chapter, it is often very hard to predict the outcome of a patent case. One of the reasons for such uncertainty is the substantial variation across judges in their interpretation of the law. In research that I conducted with Mark Schankerman, we show large dispersion in the propensity to invalidate patents across the judges at the Court of Appeal for the Federal Circuit (the US court dealing with appellate decisions for patent cases). This heterogeneity reflects different interpretation of patent laws, as well as differences in expertise and ability to process information in the various technology fields covered by patent cases.[8]

## 4.2  Non-Practicing Entities

In the past decade, a substantial volume of US patent litigation has been linked to *nonpracticing entities* (NPEs, also known as *patent trolls*). NPEs are patentees that do not produce commercial products. Their business model relies on amassing a large patent portfolio and enforcing it against alleged patent infringers. Research by Lauren Cohen, Umit Gurun, and Scott Kominers documents this trend contrasting litigation by practicing entities (PE) and non-practicing entities (NPE). They show that the increase in patent litigation due to PEs (which are firms that file patents related to the technologies they manufacture and commercialize) was modest between 2005 and 2015 relative to the one generated by NPEs.[9]

There is an intense policy debate on the effects that NPEs' patent litigation may have on innovation activity. On one side of the debate, defendants of NPEs argue that these firms are useful market intermediaries. According to this view, NPEs help small inventors to obtain returns from their patents thanks to their expertise in licensing and litigation. This is expected to be particularly valuable if the patent is infringed by well-funded large corporations, as small firms may not have the resources to litigate against these big firms. NPEs may correct this imbalance, given that the business model involves specialization in patent litigation. On the other side of the debate, opponents of NPEs claim that these firms raise the costs of innovation by gaming the legal system. According to this alternative view, NPEs are able to extract licensing revenues even when this should not take place. This can happen because the high cost of dealing with patent litigation may induce firms to pay an NPE a settlement even if they are not infringing on the patents, because the legal expenses required to prove in court that there is no infringement may exceed the amount requested by the NPE. Startup firms may be particularly vulnerable to these threats because patent litigation may reduce their chances to obtain financing or to become an acquisition target.[10]

Recently, a new business model has emerged to address the market need of protecting firms from aggressive patent litigation by NPEs: *defensive aggregators*. RPX is an example of a company operating in this space. Defensive aggregators provide a form of insurance against patent trolls, especially to large companies active in technology areas where many NPEs are present. Aggregators typically receive annual fees from subscribing companies. In exchange, they identify patents that might threaten their clients or that may help them in defending against NPE litigation, and provide licenses to these patents.[11]

## 4.3 Licensing a Patent

A license is a contract in which the owner of a patent authorizes another party to use the technology protected by the patent. Licensing deals are quite common. Survey studies show that roughly 15 percent of patents are licensed out during their lifetime.[12] Parties have a lot of flexibility when they negotiate the contractual terms of a licensing deal. For example, the license can apply nationally, or it can be restricted to a specific geographic region. It can be exclusive (no other party will be able to obtain a license) or nonexclusive. Licensing can be restricted to a particular *field of use* of the technology. For example, a patent that covers a compound useful in the treatment of various central nervous system diseases may be licensed to a firm only for the development of treatments for Alzheimer's.[13]

Patent license contracts usually include both fixed payments and royalties. *Royalties* are based on the units of product sold or some other measure of use. The most common form of royalty is a fraction of the product sales (e.g., 2 percent of revenue). However, it can also be a fixed amount per unit sold (e.g., $0.5 per product sold) or an amount linked to the total sales (e.g., $10,000 if sales are below $100,000; $25,000 if sales are between $100,000 and $1 million; and $100,000 if sales are over $1 million). *Fixed fees* are independent of sales and they are paid at specific frequencies (e.g., $50,000 per year) or when a company reaches particular *milestones*, such as developing a prototype or raising a specific amount of money from external investors. Licensing contracts may require some fixed fees to be paid upfront once the licensing deal is signed.

Sometimes startup companies pay for the license of a patent with stocks, giving up equity in their company. This is particularly common for startups founded by researchers linked to a university and using technologies patented by the university.[14]

A number of issues need to be considered when deciding whether to generate licensing revenue through royalties or through fixed fees. Royalties allow the patentee to control the market price because they affect the licensee's cost of production. From a microeconomic perspective, a royalty of $1 per unit produced is equivalent to an increase of $1 in the marginal cost of production of the licensee. This can be particularly useful when the patent is licensed to numerous firms and the licensor wants to restrict their total level of output. Fixed fees allow sharing of profits between the parties more flexibly, because they do not affect the marginal cost of production.[15] Royalties are also particularly useful for entrepreneurs and small firms that face financial constraints and cannot pay large, up-front fixed licensing fees.

Royalties allow the contractual parties to share the commercial risk of the technology. If the licensee will not be able to sell many products, the royalty payment received by the patentee will be small. Risk sharing may be an effective tool in the presence of asymmetric information, when the patentee needs to convince the licensee that the patented technology has high value. A contract that relies heavily on royalties, and thus requires low payments if the innovation does not have commercial success, may be more attractive for potential licensees.[16]

Some organizations (such as standard-setting bodies), which aim to have their patented technology widely adopted, offer licenses to an unlimited number of users on *reasonable and nondiscriminatory (RAND)* or *fair, reasonable, and nondiscriminatory (FRAND)* terms and conditions.

Patent licensing often involves more than obtaining the permission to use the technology described in the patent document. To be able to use the technology, a licensee may need additional information, such as heuristics or routines. In other words, part of knowledge required to practice the technology is *tacit* – that is, not codified in the patent document. The transfer of this tacit knowhow is an important aspect of licensing agreements, especially when the firm licensing the technology does not have a lot of experience in the technology area.[17]

After entering a licensing agreement, patentees need to ensure that the patent does not expire by paying the required maintenance fees to the patent office. Failure to pay the renewal fees may lead to the termination of the licensing contract. To ensure that the profitability of the technology is maintained, patentees should also monitor whether the patent is infringed and enforce it against alleged infringers.

## 4.4 Litigation Threat as a Driver of Licensing Revenue

In the previous two subsections, I examined patent litigation and patent licensing in isolation. In practice, these two outcomes are strongly connected because litigation can emerge when the negotiation of a license contract fails.

To illustrate more formally how the threat of patent litigation can drive licensing revenues, consider the following stylized model developed in research that I conducted with Rosemarie Ziedonis.[18] There is one firm selling a product that generates profits equal to $V$. By selling this product, the firm is potentially infringing a patent. In the absence of a license agreement, the patentee will litigate with the infringer. If litigation takes place, each firm incurs a litigation cost equal to $L$. Let us assume that the court will find the patent infringed with probability $\rho$ and not infringed with probability $1 - \rho$. If the patent is found infringed, the infringer has to halt the production and design around the infringed patent. Let us assume that this generates a loss equal to $K$. The profits of the firm when litigation takes place are

$$\pi^{Lit} = V(1 - \rho) - \rho K - L = V - \rho(K + V) - L.$$

The intuition behind the formula is the following. With probability $1 - \rho$, the court will find no infringement and the producer will enjoy profits equal to $V$. With probability $\rho$, the patent will be found infringed and the firm will sustain a loss equal to $K$. The litigation cost, equal to $L$, is paid independently of the outcome.

In the case of licensing, we indicate with $f$ the licensing fee requested by the patentee. In this case, the profits of the licensee will be

$$\pi^{Lic} = V - f.$$

The maximum license fee that will be accepted by the licensees is the fee that makes the firm indifferent between accepting and rejecting the offer, which is the $f$ at which $\pi^{Lic} = \pi^{Lit}$. Exploiting the two formulas above, it is easy to see that this fee is equal to

$$f = \rho(K + V) + L. \quad (1)$$

Equation (1) shows several drivers of the revenue that can be extracted in a patent licensing negotiation. First, the formula highlights that the rents obtained by patentees depend on the alternative to the negotiated agreement. More specifically, the fee depends on the expected outcome of the litigation taking place in the absence of licensing.[19] Licensing revenue is higher when the cost of litigation for the alleged infringer, $L$, is large. This implies that firms with a comparative advantage in litigation (e.g., because of high cash flows or access to superior legal counsel) will be able to obtain better terms in licensing deals. The parameter $L$ is usually assumed to be larger for smaller firms. Research by Josh Lerner provides evidence supporting this idea, showing that small firms avoid investing in technology fields where the threat of litigation from large firms is high.[20]

Equation (1) also suggests that the licensing fee will be larger when the strength of the patent is high and the patentee has high chances to win in court, $\rho$. Moreover, the fee is larger for technologies generating greater profits in the product market, $V$.

Finally, Equation (1) shows that the licensing fee is large when the cost of halting production, $K$, is substantial. This is the case in industries like semiconductors, where there are massive investments in clean rooms and front-end manufacturing equipment, and altering manufacturing processes is very expensive.[21]

## 4.5 Product Market Competition and Licensing Incentives

Thus far, I implicitly assumed that patent licensing was taking place between the patentee and a firm not active in the same product market as the patentee. I now discuss the case in which patentees license their technologies to product market competitors.

Research by innovation scholars Ashish Arora, Andrea Fosfuri, and Alfonso Gambardella highlights that, when an incumbent firm licenses a patent to a competitor, two key economic effects need to be considered. The first one is the *revenue effect*, which corresponds to the increase in profits that the patentee can obtain from licensing fees and royalties. Licensees must pay the patentee to access the technology, and this has a positive effect on the patentee's profits. The second one is the *rent dissipation* effect given by the drop in profits due to stronger competition in the product market. A competitor now has access to the patented technology and this tends to intensify price competition, which reduces the patentee's profits.[22]

If, after the license takes place, competition between two firms is very soft, or nonexistent, then the revenue effect will dominate the rent dissipation effect, and licensing will be profitable. Consider the case in which two firms, A and B, sell similar products in the United States and Europe. Let us assume that most of firm A's sales are in Europe and that the vast majority of firm B's sales are in the US. Firm A develops a new technology that increases the price that consumers are willing to pay for its final product relative to those sold by firm B. As long as firm A does not intend to expand its operations in the United States, licensing to firm B can be profitable because the profits of firm A in Europe will not be affected much (the rent dissipation effect is small), but large licensing revenue from sales of firm B in the United States is generated (there is a positive revenue effect). If, instead, after-licensing competition between the two firms is expected to be very intense, the rent dissipation effect may be large and induce the patentee not to license the technology.

Morton Kamien and Yair Tauman show that an industry incumbent is better off using royalties rather than fixed fees when licensing to competitors. This is because per-unit royalties, by increasing competitors' marginal costs, reduce the intensity of price competition.[23]

In some cases, licensing can be used to limit competition and sustain monopoly pricing. This can happen, for example, when firms charge each other excessive licensing royalties to artificially inflate their prices and limit the quantity of product offered in the market.[24] Alternatively, as shown in research by Nancy Gallini, a firm may aggressively license its technology to reduce the incentives of other firms to develop potentially better technologies.[25] For these reasons, patent licensing contracts and settlement of patent litigation cases can sometimes receive scrutiny by antitrust and competition authorities.

## 4.6  Patent Thickets and Cross-Licensing

During the past decades, academics and managers have noticed the emergence of *patent thickets* in several high-tech industries. As originally described by Carl Shapiro, in these technology areas, the number of patent licenses a firm requires to produce a new product is extremely large.[26] This makes it very easy for manufacturers to unintentionally infringe on a patent. Managing innovation is particularly challenging under these circumstances because firms operate under the constant threat of litigation by patentees that might lead to settlement payments, damages, or even injunctions.[27]

The semiconductor industry is one of the settings where patent thickets have been shown to be widespread. Interviews with industry sources summarized by Bronwyn Hall and Rosemary Ziedonis document that

> a given semiconductor product (say, a new memory or logic device) will often embody hundreds if not thousands of "potentially patentable" technologies that could be owned by suppliers, manufacturers in other industries, rivals, design firms, or independent inventors.[28]

Research by Rosemary Ziedonis also finds that firms operating in patent thickets tend to patent their technologies more aggressively than those operating in technology areas where IP ownership is less dispersed. This is especially the case for firms with large investments in technology-specific assets for which injunctions can be extremely costly.[29]

An IP strategy that can mitigate the problems generated by patent thickets and create some freedom to operate is to engage in *broad cross-license* agreements with other firms in the technology area. A cross-license is a contract between two firms that grants each the right to access the other's patents. In other words, it is a bilateral agreement in which two firms choose not to enforce patent rights between them. Broad cross-licenses cover the entire patent portfolios or all the patents of the two firms in some extensive technology field. In the semiconductor industry, many major industry players, such as Intel, Texas Instruments, and AMD, are involved in several broad cross-license deals.[30]

## 4.7 Patent Pools

Patent pools are agreements in which multiple patentees share patents with each other and with third parties. For example, to produce a DVD player, firms require access to a large number of patents held by various patentees. Rather than approaching each patent holder independently, from 1999 to 2020, a DVD player producer could license many of the required patents from the DVD6C patent pool, which was formed by many leading patentees (including Hitachi, Samsung, and Panasonic) and offered a one-stop shopping for all interested licensees.

Economic research has shown that the benefits of patent pooling crucially depend on the strength of the complementarity between the patents included in the pool. Pools facilitate patent licensing the most when there is strong technological complementarity between the pooled technologies and users require all the patents in the pool to commercialize a product. For example, to produce an airplane one may need to license a patent covering the design of the wings, and another covering the fuselage (body) of the aircraft. These two patents are complements because both are needed for a complete product. Conversely, two patents covering alternative wing designs are substitutes because users need only one of them to produce a working airplane.

Technological complementarity is often associated with the idea of patents being essential for the implementation of a technology standard. Assistant Attorney General Joel Klein defined essentiality:

> Essential patents, by definition, have no substitutes; one needs licenses to each of them in order to comply with the standard.[31]

Theoretical research by Josh Lerner and Jean Tirole highlights that patents are rarely perfect complements, and it is often difficult to understand whether or not a technology user can substitute a patent with another one. Moreover, technologies that are complements today may become substitutes in the future if architectural innovation leads to a change in the way in which the components of the products interact with one another.

Pools may reduce competition between patentees, and even their innovation incentives, when they include patents that are highly substitutable. This occurs because pools of substitutes constrain technology users to license patents they do not need, and this limits the incentives of patent owners to reduce their licensing fees.[32]

More recently, in the biomedical field, a different type of patent pool has emerged that aims at promoting wide geographic diffusion of specific technologies rather than aggregating complementary IP. A prominent example of such geographical patent pools is the Medicines Patent Pool (MPP) that was established in 2010 with a mandate to accelerate access to affordable HIV treatments in developing countries. The MPP negotiates patent licensing agreements with patent-holding pharmaceutical companies. For example, in July 2011, the MPP signed a license agreement with Gilead Sciences for the production of Elvitegravir, a drug for the treatment of HIV infection in adults. The agreement between Gilead and the MPP includes patents granted by 109 countries that are home to almost 90 percent of people living with HIV in low- and middle-income countries. Once a license deal with a patent holder is in place, manufacturing companies willing to produce and sell the patented product in developing countries can apply for sublicenses to the MPP. MPP patent sublicenses are nonexclusive and wide in geographical scope, covering many low- and middle-income countries.

Mark Schankerman and I conducted an empirical analysis of the impact of the MPP on patent licensing. Our research shows that the likelihood of observing at least one patent licensing deal covering a drug in a country increases substantially once the associated patent is included in the pool. The effect appears smaller in middle-income countries with high HIV incidence, which are likely to be attractive markets for pharmaceutical companies even in the absence of the MPP. Our research also shows that the MPP not only affected patent licensing but also led to greater commercialization of new drugs, which increased welfare. A study by Lucy Wang provides additional support for the beneficial effects of the pool, showing an increase in clinical trials and drug product approvals after a patent is included in the MPP.[33]

## 4.8 Compulsory Licensing

Compulsory licensing takes place when a government allows third parties to practice the technology protected by a patent without the consent of the patentee. Compulsory licensing is allowed by the WTO's agreement on intellectual property – the Trade-Related Aspects of Intellectual Property Rights (TRIPS) Agreement – in cases when negotiations for voluntary licensing fail.

Historically, compulsory licensing occurred mostly in developing countries and involved licensing of foreign technologies. For example, the governments of Brazil, Thailand, and India have used compulsory licensing to provide local manufacturers the freedom to produce HIV-related drugs. Some governments have recently considered compulsory licensing as a tool to access foreign technologies to combat climate change. Compulsory licensing has also been proposed for COVID-19 vaccines and therapeutics.

Economists Petra Moser and Alessandra Voena studied the historical case of compulsory licensing that took place in the United States after World War I. In 1918, the US Congress passed a law that licensed all US patents owned by German firms to US firms, without seeking permission from the German patentees. Their study shows that compulsory licensing was very beneficial for the growth of US firms. Thanks to this policy, American innovators were able to learn, operate, and experiment in a variety of technology fields where German firms had a technological advantage. US domestic patenting increased by about 20 percent in the areas in which patents were compulsory licensed.[34]

While compulsory licensing can be extremely beneficial for technology users, one needs to consider its possible negative impact on patentees and innovators. The risk of compulsory licensing may discourage foreign firms from transferring new technologies into developing countries, and this may lead to lower access to critical technologies. For example, when Brazil enacted a compulsory license for the HIV drug Efavirenz, the patentee, Merck, released a press statement claiming that

*this expropriation of intellectual property sends a chilling signal to re-*
*search-based companies about the attractiveness of undertaking risky research*
*on diseases that affect the developing world, potentially hurting patients who*
*may require new and innovative life-saving therapies.*[35]

## 4.9  Licensing as a Startup Commercialization Strategy

A crucial strategic decision faced by technology entrepreneurs and startups is whether to manufacture and sell their products independently or to rely on the services provided by other firms. Commercialization and manufacturing contracts often take the form of a patent license. The licensee is typically a large manufacturing company that obtains the rights to produce and sell the innovation. The patentee provides technical assistance and receives royalties or fixed fees payments from the licensee.

Research by Joshua Gans and Scott Stern emphasizes several advantages of licensing contracts as a commercialization strategy for startups and technology entrepreneurs. First, by licensing their patents, innovators avoid competing in the product market against large industry players. Large firms typically have a competitive advantage in production and commercialization, which allows them to extract larger margins than startup ventures. Patent licensing allows small innovators to tap into this advantage by collaborating with the large firms rather than competing with them. Second, engaging in patent licensing allows startup innovators to avoid big investments in manufacturing facilities and the costly acquisition of the capabilities needed for commercialization. Finally, licensing gives startups the opportunity to specialize in R&D and to spend their time and resources developing new technologies. This is particularly important for entrepreneurial teams for which research is the competitive advantage.[36]

At the same time, several factors may reduce the appeal of a licensing strategy. The first is that patent protection is often imperfect. Patent litigation may be required to stop a licensee from using the technology when contractual obligations are not met, and this can be extremely costly (or even unfeasible) for entrepreneurs and startups.

Gans and Stern also emphasize that a challenge with licensing is that identifying and accessing appropriate licensing partners can be difficult and time consuming. Large firms often receive many licensing proposals from startups and entrepreneurs. This allows large players to be very selective about technologies and partners. Venture capitalists can play an important role in facilitating a match between a startup and a larger firm.

As discussed in Section 4.3, the profits that a firm or an individual inventor can obtain from patent licensing depend on the relative bargaining power of the two negotiating parties. Several factors affect the bargaining power of a patentee in a licensing negotiation. The first is the strength of the underlying intellectual property. When patent protection is uncertain – as in some areas of software where patent invalidation rates are high – royalties will be lower. The second is the ability of the innovator to communicate and demonstrate the value of the underlying technology. Asymmetric information between the two parties about the quality of the technology may increase the risk of bargaining failure and reduce the royalties received by the patentee. Finally, startup innovators may extract high royalties in technology areas where there are multiple potential licensees, because large firms may compete to become the commercialization conduit.

## 4.10  Licensing of University Patents

Universities are a crucial source of knowledge creation. According to the National Science Board, in 2017, US academic institutions invested about $80 billion in R&D, which is about half of the total expenditure in basic research activity in the United States.[37] A key channel through which university research contributes to economic growth is through licensing the resulting inventions to private firms.[38]

In the United States, the growth in university licensing was spurred by the passage of the Bayh-Dole Act in 1980, which gave universities permission to file for patents and to grant licenses for patented inventions resulting from federally funded research. Technology licensing activity by universities increased substantially during the past decades. For example, during the years 1991–2006, the annual number of patent licenses granted by universities more than tripled, and license revenues increased from $186 million to about $1.4 billion.[39]

In most universities, intellectual property licenses are negotiated and managed by a *technology transfer office* (TTO). TTOs set intellectual property policies, which indicate how the revenue generated from licensing is split between the inventor and the university. A study by Saul Lach and Mark Schankerman provides a description of royalty sharing between inventors and universities in a sample of US academic institutions. The mean inventor's share is about 40 percent, but there is substantial variation in the data. A number of universities have royalty shares lower than a third, while the top 25 percent have royalty shares larger than 50 percent. Moreover, many universities have royalty shares that vary with the level of licensed income.[40]

The technologies licensed by universities tend to be at much earlier development stage relative to those licensed by private firms. In their survey of US universities, Jerry Thursby, Richard Jensen, and Marie Thursby found that about 50 percent of the inventions licensed were proof of concepts and that roughly 25 percent were lab scale prototypes. They also found that the vast majority of the inventions required additional involvement of the inventor to be successfully commercialized.[41]

Research has shown that the incentives to engage in patenting and technology commercialization depend substantially on the share of profits that university researchers expect to obtain from these activities. Economists Benjamin Jones and Hans Hvide have examined the effect of a large policy shift that took place in Norway in 2003. Historically, Norwegian university professors enjoyed full rights over the business ventures and the intellectual property they created. In 2003, this "professor's privilege" ended, and universities became holders of major rights on patents and startups. The study finds that this policy reform had a large negative effect on the rate at which university researchers founded startups and in the quantity and quality of university patenting.[42]

## 4.11 Patent Sales

An alternative to generating revenue through patent licensing is to sell the patent to another firm. By selling a patent, a firm gives up all its rights over the technology. This allows innovators to profit from their patents without further involvement in the commercialization of the technology. It is a strategy often pursued by firms that decide to disinvest from technology areas no longer considered "core" to their business activity. Changes in patent ownership may occur on their own or as part of larger asset sales or purchases.[43]

Research by Carlos Serrano shows that patent sales are very common. According to his estimates, individual inventors and small technology firms sell about 15 percent of their patents. Conversely, large corporations and government agencies have the lowest rates of transfer at about 10 percent and 5 percent of their patents.[44]

When ownership of the patent is transferred through a sale, the transaction needs to be recorded at the patent office. Recording the transaction protects the new patent owner against previous unrecorded transactions and subsequent sales. Data on changes in patent ownership are available through the patent offices and from search engines such as Google Patents. Technically, these records are called *patent assignments*.

## 4.12  An Alternative to Patenting: Trade Secrecy

Above, I discussed how patents can be used to manage access to a technology. Patentees can allow other firms and individuals to use their technologies with a license contract or can block them using litigation.

In the case of innovators not interested in sharing the technologies with other firms, a classic alternative to patent protection is to keep the technology secret. This strategy is quite common for startups, especially those that are cash constrained and struggle to find resources to file patent applications. In most countries, there are trade secret laws that protect innovators against misappropriation of a secret technology. Examples of misappropriation include theft and the breach of a confidentiality agreement.

Trade secret laws typically require the owner of the technology to exert some effort to conceal the technology. For example, innovators may use nondisclosure agreements and confidentiality clauses in employment contracts. They may protect the files describing the technology using encryption software or lock the printed documents in a safe.

The decision of whether to patent a technology or to keep it a secret involves considering multiple issues. First, filing patent applications can be expensive and time consuming. Secrecy allows a firm to devote its financial resources and managerial attention to other more pressing objectives.

Second, patent protection has a fixed duration, typically twenty years. Trade secrets, instead, can potentially last forever provided the technology remains a secret. A famous example of trade secret that lasted much longer than twenty years is the formula for the Coca-Cola soft drink. The document with the formula has been kept in a safe since the 1920s. Currently, the recipe lays in a vault in the company's museum in Atlanta. The vault has a palm scanner, a numerical code pad, and massive steel door. Only two senior executives know the formula at any given time.[45]

There is an important difference between product and process technologies in the effectiveness of trade secrets. It is harder to keep secret a technology embodied in a product, because customers may be able to inspect it and reverse engineer it. Process innovation – manufacturing processes in particular – that is accessible only to a few selected employees is often easier to protect through secrecy. I provide a more comprehensive discussion of the difference between product and process innovation in Chapter 6.

Trade secrets do not protect against independent discovery. Other firms and innovators that independently develop the technology can obtain a patent. Another costly aspect of trade secrecy relates to the fact that secrecy may reduce the ability of firms to describe the technology to other parties. This can be a problem because investors' willingness to invest in a firm or customers' willingness to buy a product may be reduced when they do not have complete information on the technology. This issue is particularly relevant for startup firms, because their survival may depend on successful negotiations with investors, buyers, and suppliers. Trade secrecy may also not be appropriate for research tools and other technologies whose success depends on the extent of follow-on innovation.[46]

# PART 2

# TECHNOLOGY CREATION

# CHAPTER 5

# Inducement Prizes and Open-Innovation Strategies

*At last the Dodo said, "EVERYBODY has won, and all must have prizes."*

*– Alice's Adventures in Wonderland*[1]

## 5.1 The Longitude Prize

October 22, 1707, was a tragic day in British history. That night, in stormy weather, four ships smashed into rocks near the Isles of Scilly and over 2,000 men lost their lives. The disaster was due to a miscalculation of the ships' location. In the eighteenth century, navigators were able to measure, quite accurately, their latitude (i.e., their position north or south of the equator) by observing the sun. Their position east or west of the prime meridian (their longitude) was computed, however, through "dead reckoning," a method that required estimates of the speed and distance from a given position. Wind and sea currents led to large and frequent errors in the calculation of the longitude, which could be the cause of naval disasters such as the one off the Scilly islands.

The emotional resonance of the Scilly disaster led the British Parliament to pass the Longitude Act on July 8, 1714. Three large prizes were offered for solutions to the longitude problem with different degrees of accuracy attained. A prize of £20,000 was announced for a method providing a measurement with a margin of error within one-half of a degree, £15,000 for errors within two-thirds of a degree, and £10,000 for a methodology with accuracy within one degree. To win one of the prizes, the proposed solution needed to be tested on a ship sailing

> *"over the ocean, from Great Britain to any such Port in the West Indies ... without losing their Longitude beyond the limits before mentioned"* and should be *"tried and found Practicable and Useful at Sea."*[2]

According to the leading academics at the time, the most promising approach that would lead to a solution was the lunar-distance method, which involved astronomical observation through a telescope. The strong view of the scientific elite is well summarized in a letter by Sir Isaac Newton who, commenting on the challenge, wrote, "Nothing but astronomy is sufficient for this purpose."[3]

Yet, the best solution to this challenge did not come from the academic community and did not rely on astronomy at all. It came instead from a self-taught craftsman from a small Lincolnshire village with no formal academic education. His name was John Harrison. He built his technology by exploiting the link between longitude and time. It is possible to calculate longitude based on the current time and the time at another location, usually the prime meridian in Greenwich. Sailors were able to determine the local time at sea by observing the sun. The most natural way to know the time at Greenwich was to carry on board a timekeeper set on London time. But this approach was considered unfeasible because clocks were not precise enough. Pendulum watches, which were the most reliable timekeepers at the time, could not be used on ships. Pocket watches were not accurate enough and would have generated errors as large as those obtained with "dead reckoning."

As documented in research by Gino Cattani, Simone Ferriani, and Andrea Lanza, Harrison disagreed with this view. He believed that an accurate timekeeper that would work in a marine environment could be developed, and he worked for decades to build this technology. After a few failed attempts, in 1759 he presented to the government a watch named H4. It was a pocket watch with a diameter of 5.2 inches and used jeweled bearings to minimize internal frictions and maximize accuracy. The watch was tested on a voyage from Portsmouth to Kingston, Jamaica and was found to predict the longitude with an error well below the one required to win the prize.[4]

The story of the longitude prize provides an important example of how innovation prizes can serve as powerful incentive to develop new technologies. A key feature of innovation prizes, such as the one offered by the British Parliament for the longitude problem, is that they attract a diverse set of participants who have the potential to offer solutions that can differ substantially from those provided by the dominant scientific approaches. More broadly, prizes are an example of an *open-innovation* model in which technologies are developed by reaching innovators who are outside the boundaries of the traditional research community operating in a field.

## 5.2 Inducement Prizes and the Innovation Policy Toolkit

I define *inducement prizes* as large monetary rewards paid to innovators who reach a predetermined set of performance targets. These prizes are typically paid to the first innovator who develops a technology that solves a prespecified problem. In some cases, submissions are collected up to a deadline and then the prize is paid to the best entry. Inducement prizes differ from *blue-sky prizes* (such as Nobel Prizes) granted as career recognition to researchers for innovations that are not specified in advance.[5]

Prizes are one of many innovation policies used by governments to spur research investments. In previous chapters, I discussed a different policy tool: *intellectual property (IP)*. IP differs from inducement prizes in several respects. First, IP rights are not granted for predetermined technologies. Any new technology meeting the utility, novelty, and nonobviousness requirements can be patented. Second, the reward is in the form of monopoly rights; it is not a sum of money paid directly by policymakers to innovators.

Another important innovation policy tool is the provision of *research grants*. These are monetary payments that are transferred to innovators before the technology is developed. Usually, grant applicants submit proposals to an adjudicating committee that ranks the proposals and allocates grants to the best applications. Often there are restrictions on the eligible expenses on which the grant funds can be spent. These are typically related to research costs, such as scientist salaries, lab equipment, and travel for research dissemination. There are also restrictions on the eligibility to submit a grant proposal. For example, grants from the Social Sciences and Humanities Research Council (SSHRC) are only paid to researchers affiliated to Canadian postsecondary institutions.

Research by Pierre Azoulay, Joshua Graff Zivin, Danielle Li, and Bhaven Sampat has shown that research grants provided by the public sector can have important effects on the development of new medical technologies. With a detailed analysis of the grants offered by the US National Institutes of Health (NIH), they show that $10 million in NIH funding for a research area generates 2.3 additional private-sector patents in that area.[6]

Governments also buy technologies through bilateral *research procurement contracts*. These are payments awarded to suppliers of specific technologies. Several ways are typically used to identify, negotiate, and structure the payment of these contracts. Suppliers can be paid before or after a technology is developed, or when specific technical milestones have been reached. Unlike innovation prizes, payments are often negotiated between suppliers and the government. It is common to observe restrictions in the eligibility of suppliers (e.g., only national suppliers, or firms with experience in the industry).

Countries also stimulate R&D investments through the tax code by treating these expenditures more generously than other types of capital investment, and by providing additional fiscal incentives, such as *tax credits*. More recently, governments have introduced *patent boxes*, which are lower tax rates for revenues linked to patents.

The distinction between these policy tools is often not clear-cut, and hybrid policies are sometimes used. Two features typically differentiate inducement prizes from other innovation policy instruments. The first is the nonnegotiated nature of the prize, because participants typically do not have a say in the amount adjudicated. The second one is the openness in participation. Innovators without previous experience in the technology field or preexisting connections with the government can participate, and the adjudication process usually focuses entirely on the performance of the developed technologies.

## 5.3 Inducement Prizes in the Modern Economy

The use of innovation prizes has increased substantially during the past three decades as a large number of philanthropists have launched programs aimed at rewarding the development of socially valuable technologies. The Gates Foundation, Qualcomm, and Nokia are examples of organizations that have offered multimillion-dollar prizes for children's immunization and the development of affordable medical devices.[7]

One of the drivers of the increase in the use of prizes was the success of a contest run by Peter Diamandis, who in 1996 offered a $10 million prize to the first privately financed team that could build and fly a three-passenger vehicle 100 kilometers into space twice within two weeks. On October 4, 2004, this challenge, named the Ansari XPrize, was won by Mojave Aerospace Ventures (a team led by Burt Rutan, a pioneering space engineer, and Paul Allen, co-founder of Microsoft). The contest motivated 26 teams from seven nations to invest more than $100 million in pursuit of the $10 million purse.[8] The large amount of R&D investment generated (ten times the prize amount!) stimulated interest in innovation challenges from private firms and governments alike.

Former US President Obama's Strategy for American Innovation strongly encouraged the use of innovation prizes, and the America Competes Reauthorization Act of 2011 provided all federal agencies the power to offer innovation prizes.[9] Since then, the US government has implemented more than 1,000 challenges in more than 100 federal agencies.

One of the most successful examples of an innovation prize run by a public agency is the 2004 DARPA Grand Challenge in which a $1 million prize was offered to the team that built a self-driving car that drove the fastest through 150 miles of the Mojave Desert. The prize was offered by the Defense Advanced Research Projects Agency (DARPA) with the goal of obtaining technologies useful for the US defense sector, which was looking to make ground military forces autonomous. This DARPA challenge is often described as the innovation contest that jump-started the self-driving car industry.[10]

Since 2009, the National Aeronautics and Space Administration (NASA) started offering a variety of innovation prizes through global open-innovation platforms such as Innocentive and Top-coder. NASA challenges have spanned a large variety of technologies, including heliophysics, mechanical engineering, radiation, material science, microbiology, and medical devices. NASA awards have led to successful technologies despite being small relative to the R&D budget of the agency (about $15,000 to $30,000 per prize).[11]

## 5.4  Advance Market Commitments

*Advance market commitments* (AMCs) are an important class of innovation prizes that have recently been used to incentivize the development of vaccines for diseases affecting some of the poorest countries on the planet.[12]

In an AMC, the prize organizer specifies technical requirements for the innovation and also links the payment to specific observable market outcomes. For example, a government may offer an AMC for the development of a vaccine for a disease and pay a 10-million-dollar prize only if the clinical trials are successful and at least 2 million doses are sold at 50 cents each. Notice that this is equivalent to a price top-up of $5 per dose for the first 2 million doses sold.

This top-up provides a financial return for the innovator and removes part of the deadweight loss that would have been generated by monopoly pricing (assuming that a monopolist would price each dose above 50 cents). At the same time, conditioning the payment to a level of demand ensures that the developed vaccine meets the needs of the country.

This class of prizes involves a "commitment" component that helps to address possible concerns of the innovators that the R&D investment might not be profitable because consumers lack sufficient income to generate significant revenue. The "market" component of the AMC is that the prize is only paid when the low-income country purchases enough units through a small copayment. This feature helps to avoid paying a prize to firms that develop technologies meeting the technical specifications but are not attractive to consumers for reasons that were overlooked in the prize specification.[13]

Michael Kremer, Jonathan Levin, and Christopher Snyder provide a theoretical analysis of the optimal AMC design. A key insight from their study is that policymakers should consider how far along the technology is in its development cycle when designing an AMC. For "late-stage" technologies, for which the R&D stage is almost completed, the key goal of the policymaker should be to spur investment in production capacity. In the case of "early-stage" technologies, the main goal of the AMC sponsor should be to induce R&D investments in addition to capacity building. This implies that the total amount of money required for the AMC is larger in the case of early-stage technologies. Moreover, for early-stage innovations, country copayments play a crucial role as "kill switch" devices for products providing little consumer welfare.[14]

In June 2009, the Bill & Melinda Gates Foundation partnered with a variety of governments to implement an AMC for the development of a vaccine against pneumococcal diseases prevalent in developing countries. The total prize award was $1.5 billion, which led to the development and provision of vaccines in several poor countries.[15]

## 5.5 Participating in a Challenge

Innovation prizes run across the world in the past decades have shown that challenges can be an effective way of attracting a large number of innovators to work on a technological problem. While the cash reward is an important driver of participation, the innovation management literature has also emphasized a variety of additional reasons why individuals and teams participate in innovation challenges.

Participants may value the media attention that comes with being part of the prize competition. Innovation challenges may also introduce innovators to a new community and generate networking and career opportunities. In many cases, interacting and observing the technology developed by other participants may provide valuable educational and learning opportunities. There is also a fun component to being part of a challenge.

In their detailed analysis of the Progressive Insurance Automotive XPrize for the development of super fuel-efficient vehicles, Fiona Murray, Scott Stern, Georgina Campbell, and Alan MacCormack discuss the development of an industry reputation as a crucial factor driving participation. In one of the interviews reported in the study, one of the prize participants stated,

> We're a new company ... we don't have a history for consumers to base their assessment of our vehicle's reliability or durability. XPRIZE gave us the opportunity for third-party validation of the claim of being the most energy efficient.

Another participant stated,

> It gave us a very rigid timetable ... As very small, lean company, that is challenging. If you are Ford or GM and you are on a strict deadline-you throw more people on the project. We don't have those numbers which forces us to be smarter. ... When engineers are left up to their own devices, they can iterate themselves into oblivion.

This comment highlights a potential role that prize competitions may have as a discipline device for startup companies.[16]

These benefits need to be contrasted with the potential cost of taking part in a challenge, especially when participants are startup companies. Participating in a contest is a high-risk endeavor, because only the best technology wins the award. Moreover, participation implies diverting resources from other business activities, and this may have important budget implications. Finally, the media attention and the industry reputation effects generated by participation in a challenge may not necessarily be positive. If the technology of the company fails miserably at the challenge, this may have serious long-term consequences for the way the company and its products are perceived.

## 5.6  Organizing an Innovation Challenge

A central class of problems in the economics of innovation literature examines how a sponsor should design an innovation prize. The challenges involved are numerous.

First, one must set the right size of cash award. A prize that is too large may lead to overpayment for the technology and the waste of resources. This can be especially problematic when the monetary award is paid using taxpayer money and overpayment may generate political backlash. On the other hand, an award that is too small may reduce the incentives to participate in the challenge, invest in innovation, and develop the technology.

Another challenging problem is deciding whether to allocate multiple prizes or only a single prize. One of the first to ask this question was Sir Francis Galton, who in 1902 wrote,

> A certain sum, say £100, is available for two prizes to be awarded at a forthcoming competition; the larger one for the first of the competitors, the smaller one for the second. How should the £100 be most suitably divided between the two? What ratio should a first prize bear to that of a second one? Does it depend on the number of competitors, and if so, why?[17]

About 100 years later, economists Benny Moldovanu and Aner Sela provided a mathematical answer to this difficult question.[18] They show that in a large class of economic environments, it is optimal for the organizer to allocate all the purse to a single prize. This is especially the case when the organizer cares not only about the best solution submitted by the participants but also about generating a general increase in innovation activity in the technology field. According to their analysis, awarding several prizes may be optimal only in a few instances, typically when the R&D costs required to improve the technology tend to increase more than proportionally (i.e., they are convex). In this case, the precise distribution of prizes depends in a complex way on the rate at which the R&D costs increase and the distribution of R&D productivity of the potential participants.

Sponsors may also need to assess whether the number of participants is adequate. In an empirical analysis of software innovation contests, Kevin Boudreau, Nicola Lacetera, and Karim Lakhani show that an increase in the number of competitors generates two opposite effects. First, entry stimulates greater competition, which reduces the incentives of each participant to exert effort and make investments. On the other hand, adding competitors increases the likelihood that at least one participant will find an extreme-value solution. Their analysis shows that the effort-reducing effect of greater rivalry is more dominant for less uncertain technology problems. In this case, the prize organizer may prefer to avoid excessive entry. Conversely, the extreme-value effect prevails for more uncertain problems.[19]

Specifying ex-ante the technical features required of the winning technologies is probably the most challenging aspect of prize design. For example, the goal of the Progressive Insurance Automotive X Prize was the development of vehicles able to

> *inspire a new generation of the absolute best, viable, super fuel-efficient vehicles that meet consumer expectations for safety and performance.*[20]

Translating broad goals like this one into precise requirements for a contest is extremely difficult. While technical metrics are required to set a target for the prize, the future impact of the technology may be related to characteristics that are difficult to specify in advance with unambiguous criteria.

The Progressive Insurance Automotive XPrize required vehicles to meet an efficiency standard of 100 MPGe (miles per gallon or energy equivalent) with $CO_2$ emissions equivalent to < 200 g/mi. However, statements from the XPrize Foundation indicate that the overall impact of the technology on consumers and follow-on innovation was unlikely to depend on fuel efficiency alone. Other dimensions related to the manufacturing process and consumer desirability would also be very important components of the welfare generated by the innovation. For example, research by Fiona Murray and her coauthors highlights how organizers were worried that hyperefficient cars often "look like rolling coffins" and wanted to make sure that the winning vehicles would appeal consumers.[21]

In research that I conducted with Matthew Mitchell and Gabor Virag, we explain how the allocation of intellectual property rights to participants can help to deal with this class of problems. Because only a subset of innovative activities can be measured and contracted for, a challenge that only pays monetary awards may induce the participants to disregard and to underinvest in the features of the technology not specified in the prize. When winning teams obtain not only the cash award but also full ownership of their patent rights, this underinvestment may be reduced.[22] This is exactly what happens in XPrize contests because participants are allowed to keep the IP rights on their technologies.

Innovation prizes may also be a natural setting where the organizer does not have the ability to make credible, or enforceable, promises about the payment of a prize. The story of the longitude prize is perhaps the most legendary example of the commitment problems associated with inducement prizes. Harrison encountered numerous obstacles in his dealings with the Board of Longitude, and a full forty-seven years elapsed before Harrison actually received the prize award.

More recently, several prize advocates have emphasized the idea that commitment is crucial to the success of innovation prizes. For example, Michael Kremer and Rachel Glennerster highlight how prizes for the development of vaccines stimulate R&D only if contest participants believe that the sponsor will not renege once the desired products have been developed and R&D costs have been sunk.[23] Issues of the commitment to and credibility of prizes were also discussed in the press in 2013, when the XPrize Foundation canceled a prize for the design of a device that sequenced 100 human genomes in less than thirty days.[24]

The issues of commitment and credibility highlight an important tension between the open and free entry nature of prizes from the perspective of participants relative to the limited number of organizations that have the resources and reputation required to organize and run an innovation challenge.[25]

A final issue relates to the potential biases of the adjudicating committees, which may lead to higher chances of winning the awards for specific categories of technologies and participants even if the submitted inventions are not economically important. This has been shown in several historical settings, such as the longitude prize, where the committee expected a different type of technology to win. In a comprehensive study of innovation prizes awarded by the British Royal Society in the eighteenth century, economic historian Zorina Khan shows that the awards went disproportionately to members of the British elite. She reports that one of the missions of the adjudicating committee was to decry the *vulgar and gaudy* tastes of the consumers and to engage in consumer education so that *no manufacturer will have to complain that their best productions are left in their hands, and their worst preferred.* Assessing the presence of these (implicit or explicit) biases is crucial when designing an innovation challenge.[26]

## 5.7 The Crowd as an Innovation Partner

Innovation contests are an example of an open-innovation strategy. In an open-innovation model, a firm develops and commercializes ideas generated outside of its boundaries.[27] In Chapter 4, I discussed the case in which a firm was able to use the technology developed by someone else through a patent-licensing contract. In the case of innovation prizes, the prize organizer opens the idea-generation process to a bigger crowd of innovators.

When technology solutions are submitted by a large number of external inventors, as in the case of an innovation prize, one should expect the quality of the best submitted idea to increase in the number of submitted solutions. Crucially, even if the quality of the average idea falls with the increase in the number of submissions, the quality of the best solution is likely to increase. This is particularly the case when there is substantial variance in the underlying quality of technologies submitted by prize participants. This has important implications for corporate managers because it suggests that it is not necessarily optimal to rely on a pool of well-known experts to obtain new technologies, and that there are advantages to drawing from a larger and diverse pool of participants.

Building on these insights, management scholars Andrew King and Karim Lakhani have developed a framework that helps managers choose among a variety of open-innovation strategies.[28]

In an innovation prize, such as the XPrizes discussed above, external participants submit ideas (solutions) to the organizer who then selects the best idea submitted by the participants. In this case, *idea selection* is kept internal whereas *idea generation* is open.

An alternative approach is to open the idea-selection process but not the idea-generation process. This *approval contest* strategy typically takes the form of polling consumers. It is a very common strategy in clothing and fashion. LEGO, the Danish toy company, often asks consumers to vote on product ideas that will guide their decisions to sell future model kits. This can generate significant value when outsiders have distinctive expertise and perspectives, which enable them to pick winning ideas.

Finally, managers may consider opening the innovation process for both the idea generation and idea selection. An example is the online clothing platform Threadless, where users submit designs for new products and rate the designs submitted by other members of the community. Through this type of open-innovation strategy, a company coordinates an *open-innovation community* that generates new products and identifies market opportunities with the greatest potential. As I will discuss in the next section, these communities are common in the software industry in the form of open-source coding projects.

Determining the right open-innovation strategy is a complex problem that requires considering a variety of issues. King and Lakhani emphasize the importance of the following key aspects. The first one is whether the knowledge needed to solve an innovation problem is concentrated within a few individuals or firms or is broadly dispersed among a large number of innovators. Second, managers should consider whether there are obstacles that prevent industry outsiders from participating in the innovation process. Opening the idea-generation process may be valuable when one expects many external innovators to be willing to contribute. Managers should then consider whether outside innovators also have unique knowledge about customer needs and market trends. If this is the case, opening the idea selection process can be valuable.

## 5.8 Open-Source Software

One of the most prominent examples of open-innovation community is open-source software. The history of open-source begins in 1983 when Richard Stallman launched GNU, a project aimed at developing the first fully open operating system. Stallman developed the code, which was then distributed through a license known as GNU General Public License, or GPL, guaranteeing freedom to use, study, modify, and share the source code.[29]

Many programmers built on Stallman's idea. The most important contribution came from Linus Torvalds, who created the Linux operating system in 1991. The flexibility provided by this system led to a large diffusion of Linux in the early 2000s, when it was adopted by leading organizations like NASA, Dell, and IBM. The mobile operating system Android (commercially sponsored by Google) is also open-source and based on a modified version of Linux.

Open-source communities operate on a variety of platforms. Currently, the largest one is GitHub (owned by Microsoft), with about 40 million developers working on open-source projects across the globe.

Many studies in management literature have investigated the reasons for developers to operate in open-source communities. These studies distinguish between intrinsic and extrinsic motives. *Intrinsic motives* relate to personal enjoyment, namely how creative a person feels when working on a project. *Extrinsic motives* refer to external benefits, such as peer recognition, which can generate career advancement and future job offers. There are also learning benefits that someone can obtain from contributing to an open-source project. Coders can improve their programming skills and compare their performance with those of top coders. In some cases, open-source work is actually paid. For example, GitHub recently started to collect donations from sponsors to pay developers operating on the platform.

Sharon Belenzon and Mark Schankerman examined empirically the key drivers of contribution to open-source projects. Their central finding is that there is sorting between projects and developers, and that this sorting is strongly related to the underlying motivations of the coders. Coders who are primarily motivated by the ideology of the open-source movement almost exclusively contribute to projects that are less likely to generate commercial gain. Conversely, coders who are driven by reputational gains and career concerns appear to contribute primarily to larger projects with more commercial value.[30]

A final question is how a company is able to profit from an open-source strategy. Firms generate revenues from open-source codes in different ways. One option is to charge a price for software installation and support. Alternatively, one can offer upgraded versions of the products by subscription (dual licensing) or provide an open-source core of the software but require payments for add-ons. Finally, companies like Google profit from the Android system through ad-sponsored apps and data collected from users.

Josh Lerner and Mark Schankerman document how firms comingle open-source and traditional proprietary software. In their analysis of the software industry, they find that it is very common for firms to develop both open-source and proprietary software. As they put it, "mixing is the rule not the exception." This important finding indicates that firms can leverage substantial product development and commercialization synergies between open-source and proprietary software. The appropriate mixture of the two types of software varies across companies and economic conditions. Larger firms appear more likely to engage in some open-source software but are less likely to fully specialize in it.[31]

It is important to notice that users of open-source software need to enter a licensing agreement with the developer. Open-source licenses require the source code and the program to be available for distribution at little or no charge. Multiple types of open-source licenses are used in practice, which differ in the extent to which they allow contributors to profit from their code.

Josh Lerner and Jean Tirole classify open-source licenses into three categories. The first is *highly restrictive licenses*, such as GPL. These licensing contracts prohibit the mixing of open source and private code in distributed work and require all derivative work of GPL code to be subject to GPL. The second category is *restrictive licenses,* such as the lesser general public license (LGPL) that allow developers some flexibility in mixing the code with non-open-source programs. The third group includes the *unrestrictive licenses,* such as the MIT license, the Berkeley Software Distribution (BSD) license and the Apache license. The terms of these licenses grant substantial freedom to use the software in commercial applications.[32]

Josh Lerner and Jean Tirole also developed a theoretical framework that can help developers to choose the appropriate open-source license type for their software. Their model suggests that permissive licenses (such as MIT or BSD licenses) should be preferable for projects that have strong appeal to the community of open-source contributors. These are projects where the community of developers can benefit substantially from tailoring the code to their own projects. Restrictive licenses instead are typically more appropriate for projects geared toward end users (such as games and desktop applications). Restrictive licenses may also be appropriate when the community perceives a high risk of "hijacking" by commercial firms. Hijacking occurs when a firm adds proprietary code to the open-source software and creates a successful proprietary derivative work that has the potential to dominate the market.[33]

# CHAPTER 6

# Innovation Incentives

*Ideas are like rabbits. You get a couple and learn how to handle them, and pretty soon you have a dozen.*

– John Steinbeck[1]

## 6.1 The Drivers of Innovation

How can firms reach their full innovative potential? Does the business environment affect firms' innovation outcomes? These are two defining questions for the field of innovation management. While there are still many unknowns about the determinants of innovation success, in the past decades, economics and management scholars identified several factors that have important effects on the innovation activity of small and large firms.

In this chapter, I will provide an overview of some of the most important forces driving the creation of technology capital identified in the literature. I will begin examining the role of monetary incentives and compensation schemes offered to employees engaged in the development of new technologies. I will then discuss the effects of managerial beliefs, corporate culture, and the ability of firms to keep track of the latest scientific discoveries in their technology fields. My analysis will also examine how the size of the firm and the competitive pressure in the industry can shape research investments. I will conclude by discussing the process of creative destruction and how firm innovation success may be undermined by the development of new radical technologies.

As suggested by John Steinbeck in the epigraph of this chapter, the innovation process can be managed. Before embarking in the discussion of how to manage it, I provide some terminology and notation that will be used throughout the rest of the book.

## 6.2 Taxonomy of Innovation

The academic literature identifies various categories of innovation.

The first distinction is between *product innovation* and *process innovation*. This taxonomy was initially introduced by Jacob Schmookler, who defined product innovation as technologies that lead to the creation of new or substantially improved products. Conversely, process innovation relates to improvements in manufacturing processes. Consider the case of a car manufacturer, such as Ford, Honda, or BMW. From their perspective, a new model of car is a product innovation, while a new assembly robot that reduces the cost of production of existing car models would be a process innovation.

Microeconomic theory provides an effective formula to capture the distinction between product and process innovation. In economics, firm profits are typically modeled by a simple difference between sales revenue and production costs. Revenue is computed multiplying the quantity of product sold with the price charged per unit of product.

Economists typically indicate the total quantity of product sold with $q$ and the price charged with $p$. More specifically, the price charged is mathematically modeled as a decreasing function of the quantity sold: $p(q)$. The negative slope of the function is a natural assumption because it captures the idea that a firm needs to charge a lower price to sell larger quantities of product, everything else equal. A simple extension of this model is to assume that the price is a function of two variables: the quantity sold, $q$, and quality of the product, $\theta$. In this case we would indicate the price with the function $p(q,\theta)$ which decreases in $q$ (the larger the quantity of product in the market the lower its price) and increases in $\theta$ (firms can charge higher prices for higher quality products).

The cost of production is typically denoted as $cq$, where the parameter $c$ captures the per-unit cost of production. Building on this notation, we can write the profits of the firm, $\pi$, as

$$\pi = p(q,\theta)q - cq$$

where the first component of the formula indicates the sales revenue, and the second component captures the production costs. The primary effect of product innovations is to increase $\theta$. They increase firm profits because they lead to higher quality products, which generate more revenue because the willingness to pay of consumers is higher. Process innovations are innovations that mainly reduce $c$. They increase a firm's profits by reducing the production costs of the firm.

The distinction between product and process innovation is important because managers may need to complement the adoption of a new technology with other strategic decisions. For example, product innovation may require new marketing strategies related to pricing and advertising. More generally, assessing whether or not a new product should be developed requires an understanding of the value that customers place on quality improvement and its impact on market prices. Conversely, process innovation may require changes in labor force composition. Strategic decisions related to the development and adoption of new manufacturing technologies require an understanding of the skills needed to operate the new equipment.

In practice, distinguishing between product and process innovation is not easy. For example, a new robot used to manufacture cars is a production process from the perspective of a car manufacturer, but it is a final product from the perspective of a robot producer. Moreover, the introduction of new products often leads to changes in production costs, because producing higher-quality products typically costs more than producing lower-quality products. In some cases, high-quality products substantially increase the market demand for the innovating firms, which in turn leads to investments into cost-reducing processes. As I will discuss in Chapter 8, technologies related to safety aspects of products can jointly have properties of product and process innovations.

There are substantial differences in the amount of product and process innovation across industries. For example, about three-quarters of new technologies developed in petroleum refining are process innovation, whereas less than one-quarter of new pharmaceutical technologies are process innovation.[2]

A second common taxonomy distinguishes between *incremental* and *radical* innovation. Incremental innovation refers to the introduction of a relatively minor change to existing products or processes. A radical innovation instead involves a substantial improvement of the technology. Often a radical improvement is based on newly developed engineering and scientific principles.[3]

Rather than focusing on whether the innovation mainly affects revenue or costs, the distinction between radical and incremental innovation focuses on the magnitude of the change in profits. Consider the case of a process innovation. Let us call $c_0$ the production cost before the innovation and $c_1$ the cost with the new technology, with $c_1 < c_0$. Whether the process innovation is radical or incremental depends on the magnitude of the cost reduction, $c_0 - c_1$, with incremental technologies associated with relatively minor changes in cost. A similar point can be made for product innovation, because radical technologies tend to be associated with large changes in quality $\theta_1 - \theta_0$.

In the context of product innovation, it is important to assess not only the extent of the improvement in technical performance, but also how much the consumers' willingness to pay changes. Sometimes, new products that are substantially different from existing devices from an engineering perspective are not perceived as radically different by consumers. In other words, large technical product improvements, that is, large $\theta_1 - \theta_0$, may still generate minor changes in their willingness to pay, that is, small $p(q,\theta_1) - p(q,\theta_0)$.

In the economics literature, radical innovation sometimes is called "drastic" innovation. Nobel laureate Kenneth Arrow provided one of the first economic definitions of "drastic" process innovation. According to his definition, drastic process innovation is such that the price that a monopolist would charge with the new technology does not exceed the competitive price under the old technology. In other words, the cost reduction generated by a drastic innovation is so large that if a single firm owns the new technology and behaves as a monopolist, no other firm with the old technology would be able to earn profits.[4]

Radical technologies have received particular attention in the economics and management literatures because they have the potential to overturn existing market structures when the new technology is superior to current practices and diffuses rapidly. Take, for example, the development of digital photography, which replaced film cameras, or the DVD, which replaced VHS. These innovations led to the emergence of new industry segments and strongly challenged the competitive advantage of the firms that had dominated the industries with the older technologies.

The economics and management literatures have developed several other taxonomies of innovation. *Architectural* innovation refers to innovations changing the way in which the components of a product are linked together, while leaving the core design concepts (and thus the basic knowledge underlying the components) untouched.[5] Conversely, a *component* innovation results in changes of components of the system without altering the overall design of the product. Innovations are also classified as *competence-enhancing* or *competence-destroying*, depending on whether or not they build on a firm's existing knowledge and skills.

## 6.3 The Role of Monetary Incentives

How much should the compensation of scientists depend on the success of their research projects? To examine this question, let us begin with two technical definitions. Economists refer to *high-powered* incentives as compensation schemes that depend substantially on the success/failure of a project. Examples include pay-for-performance contracts and bonuses received by the employees in case of successful outcomes. Conversely, *low-powered* incentives are compensation schemes that are not strongly related to the outcome of a work project. A classic example is a fixed monthly wage.

Many research institutions pay their personnel mainly using low-powered incentives. Most universities, for example, tend to pay their senior researchers a fixed yearly salary, and bonuses linked to research productivity are rare and often small.[6] Fixed compensations and low bonuses are common in the private sector too. History is full of examples of successful technologies developed by employees under a low-powered incentive scheme. As documented by Josh Lerner, Percy Spencer, who invented the microwave oven in 1945, obtained only $2 from the discovery. Similarly, Shuji Nakamura, a research scientist at the Japanese firm Nichia, discovered in 1993 the blue light-emitting diode, a technology that generated over one billion dollars in profits to the company. The inventor's bonus for this discovery was only $180.[7]

In a detailed analysis of the compensation of the heads of research and development departments of large corporations, Josh Lerner and Julie Wulf show that US firms were reluctant to use high-powered incentives in the 1980s. Their analysis also shows that this changed dramatically over the course of the 1990s, with much greater use of high-powered incentives, especially restricted stock units and stock options. They show that the ratio of the value of high-powered incentives to cash compensation for corporate R&D heads more than doubled during this time. More importantly, Lerner and Wulf's study finds that the use of high-powered incentives generated positive effects on firms' innovation, especially among companies with centralized R&D organizations. Greater use of stock options and restricted stock were associated with more heavily cited patents. This finding suggests that the use of high-powered incentives can be a powerful strategy to reward innovation.[8]

At the same time, the economics literature has identified settings where pay-for-performance may backfire and not be an effective way to stimulate innovation. These are typically environments characterized by *multitasking*, which is a term capturing the idea that workers need to perform multiple activities to successfully complete a project. In these settings, it is often the case that some of the activities can be easily monitored, whereas other tasks cannot be measured or tracked. This implies that bonuses can be easily linked to the measurable aspects of the performance but cannot be linked to other aspects, which are more difficult to track or describe. The literature has shown that in cases where many important activities are hard to measure or describe, it may make sense to offer compensation schemes with flat or very limited sensitivity to performance. This is because high-powered incentives may lead workers to focus only on measurable tasks and neglect other valuable activities.

In the context of technology development, examples of measurable outcomes are the number of new patents filed or the number of scientific articles published. Motorola, for example, implemented a policy that rewarded its engineers for filing patents, with bonuses of several thousand dollars.[9] Such compensation schemes may backfire because they induce the researcher to focus exclusively on getting the bonus and to overlook other research activities, even if they might be very valuable to the firm. For example, the researcher may file many low-value patents or publish many articles with low impact rather than working on more ambitious and risky projects. Moreover, bonuses tied to individual productivity may lead researchers to collaborate less and not to share preliminary research findings with colleagues and team members.

Theoretically, therefore, it is not clear whether high-powered incentives are likely to work in stimulating innovative effort. Designing the compensation scheme for creative workers, such as engineers and scientists, is a complex task. An important recent contribution providing some guidance in this respect is the microeconomic analysis by Gustavo Manso. Manso argues that compensation schemes that motivate innovation should be more complex than standard pay-for-performance contracts. This is because the development of new technologies, especially the most radical ones, requires exploration of new scientific concepts and may have very high risk of failure. Standard pay-for-performance contracts punish innovators if their projects fail. This may have negative effects on research incentives because researchers may prefer to focus on simpler projects that are less likely to fail. According to Manso, an effective compensation scheme requires substantial tolerance (or even reward) for early failure as well as reward for long-term success. Manso also suggests that job security and timely feedback on performance are essential to motivate innovators.[10]

Empirical support for the insights of Manso is provided in a study by Pierre Azoulay, Joshua Graff Zivin, and Gustavo Manso, who compare different institutions funding scientific research and show that those with tolerance for short-term failure and evaluation based on long-term results are more effective at motivating scientific research.[11]

Research by Philippe Aghion, John Van Reenen, and Luigi Zingales also provides support for this idea in the corporate setting, showing that when CEOs are less likely to be dismissed after a decline in profits, as in the case of institutional ownership, companies appear more innovative. Results consistent with Manso's theory have also been found in laboratory experiments.[12]

## 6.5  Managerial Beliefs and Innovation

A substantial body of applied psychology literature shows that individuals often overestimate their skills. For example, many people tend to believe they are talented drivers, or that they have superior ability to remember trivia.[13] This literature also shows that corporate CEOs and other high-ranking executives are particularly susceptible to this bias. In fact, overconfidence tends to be stronger among highly skilled individuals, especially when the link between actions and outcomes is complex. These are features that characterize many senior executives and their daily activities.

Using data on CEOs' personal financial decisions, economists Ulrike Malmandier and Geoffrey Tate developed an empirical measure of CEO overconfidence.[14] Exploiting this measure, the finance literature found that hiring overconfident CEOs may have negative effects on corporations. More specifically, this line of research has shown that one of the main problems with overconfident CEOs is that they often destroy value through unprofitable mergers and suboptimal investment behavior.[15] Despite these negative effects, many companies hire and retain overconfident CEOs. Why do they do that?

My research with Timothy Simcoe addresses this issue, showing that for large-firm CEOs, overconfidence is associated with an increased propensity to innovate. Our analysis shows that the arrival of an overconfident CEO is associated with a 25 to 35 percent increase in the number of patents filed by the firms as well as in their quality. The finding suggests that the greater research productivity of overconfident CEOs may offset the negative impacts of executive overconfidence found in previous research.[16]

An example of an overconfident CEO in our sample is Donald Fites, who ran Caterpillar from 1990 to 1999. He often revealed his confidence in the press and in his writing with statements like "We think we are better engineers and manufacturers than our competitors."[17] Indeed, the innovation performance of Caterpillar improved substantially during his tenure.

More broadly, this line of work suggests that CEOs' attitudes and beliefs may have very important effects on their firms' innovative performance. Innovation involves experimentation, exploration, and risk-taking. From this perspective, risk-averse leaders and senior executives with pessimistic views may not allow a firm to achieve its full innovation potential. Confidence and positive attitudes may instead spur exploration of new technological opportunities. At the same time though, one has to remember that overconfidence may reduce value through other channels identified in the literature, such as excessive mergers and acquisitions. Even in the case of innovation, it may be possible that overconfidence leads a CEO to overinvestment or to poor project selection.

## 6.6  Innovative Organizational Culture

Organizational culture consists of the set of managerial values and social behaviors that define the way a firm operates. The culture of a firm is a key driver of the way suppliers, customers, and employees are treated.[18]

A substantial volume of research and case studies has examined what the key characteristics of an innovative corporate culture are. A recent book by Gary Pisano provides an extensive analysis of the main findings and prescriptions from this line of research, emphasizing the trade-offs involved in creating a corporate culture conducive to innovation.[19] The following are three of the most important aspects identified by Pisano.

The first one is *tolerance for failure but not for incompetence*. Innovative companies allow employees to experiment and tolerate failures, especially for the most risky and ambitious research projects. At the same time, tolerance for failure needs to be accompanied by strong performance standards. Companies fail if they are too tolerant, in the sense of accepting sloppy execution or failures in activities that are easy to perform.

The second feature is *extensive but disciplined experimentation*. Organizations with strong research records are constantly experimenting with new technological paths and exploring ideas for new products and processes. But experimentation has its costs too, because it can lead to persistent uncertainty and ambiguity. Research projects suffer if they are constantly kept in the experimentation phase. The most innovative companies are those that design and select experiments extremely carefully. Moreover, they have processes in place to decide when to stop experimenting and either discontinue a project or implement it full scale.

Third, Pisano highlights that innovative organizations tend to be *both collaborative and individually accountable*. Team collaboration is an important driver of innovation success because groups can share technical knowledge and are more likely to consider diverse approaches when facing technical challenges. At the same time, to rely excessively on groups may slow down the decision-making process, because team consensus is often required. Moreover, group projects may induce individuals to contribute less because the success of the project and their recognition depend less on their individual efforts. This is what economists call the *free-riding* problem. Innovative firms mitigate these problems by introducing some individual accountability. For example, they implement a system where groups and committees are formed to provide input and feedback, but specific individuals are responsible for making the most critical choices.

Pisano also discusses how innovative cultures tend to blend psychological safety with the provision of frank feedback and to have strong leaders but not extremely hierarchical organizations. Overall, Pisano's analysis highlights that developing an innovative culture can be extremely challenging. There are important cost–benefit trade-offs that management needs to understand. Tolerance for failure is important, but excessive tolerance may backfire. Developing new technologies requires extensive experimentation, but continuous and unmanaged experimentation will not reach any goal. The key implication of Pisano's analysis is that balancing these aspects is hard, which is one of the key reasons why corporations with successful innovation culture are not common.

## 6.7  Absorptive Capacity

Successful research pushes the technology frontier forward. An important requirement for generating new knowledge is the ability to understand where the research frontier lies, and to identify open questions and new research paths to explore. In other words, the creation of new knowledge requires the capacity to assimilate and exploit existing external knowledge.

This point was made by Wesley Cohen and Daniel Levinthal in an influential paper that introduced the idea of *absorptive capacity*.[20] These scholars argued that it is costly for firms to access and understand the knowledge produced outside their boundaries. Even when this knowledge is in the public domain – as in the case of many scientific results generated by universities – understanding it, assimilating it, and potentially using it in new R&D projects requires costs in terms of effort, expertise, and time. This argument implies that a new scientific discovery will not provide equal benefits to all firms operating in the technology area and that the benefits enjoyed by firms will be determined by their own actions, capabilities, and resources.

The management literature has examined a number of strategies that firms can follow to build such absorptive capacity. For example, managers should make sure that R&D personnel have exposure to external knowledge through participation in scientific conferences and access to the latest scientific publications.

In practice, many companies engage in "pure" scientific research that leads to publication in scientific journals and knowledge shared with the broad academic community. Historically, many significant scientific breakthroughs have come from scientists who were not working in universities but in corporate labs owned by companies, such as AT&T, Du Pont, and IBM. The development of absorptive capacity is one of the reasons why these firms engage in scientific research. Other explanations for corporate science include attracting and incentivizing the best scientist-inventors,[21] and increasing the firms' reputation to attract investors and customers.[22]

Ashish Arora, Sharon Belenzon, and Lia Sheer provide a theoretical and empirical analysis suggesting that, in deciding how much to invest in corporate science, managers face an important trade-off. The more they can use their scientific discovery internally to stimulate the development of new products, the more valuable is the investment in basic science. At the same time, there may be costs associated with research findings "spilling over" to rivals, that is, they can stimulate innovation of rivals and the development of competing products.[23]

Another important channel through which firms can learn the latest scientific developments is through collaboration with universities in basic research projects. Firms that collaborate with universities have been shown to have higher innovation performance and to develop higher quality technologies at a faster pace.[24] Collaborations with university scientists can help firms to identify the most relevant new scientific research. Moreover, in many cases, reading a published article may not provide sufficient knowledge to understand and exploit the underlying scientific finding. On-going collaborations with universities allow firms to access unpublished or tacit knowledge required to fully use such scientific results.

An important implication from this line of research is that it can be very dangerous for a firm to operate under an insular research culture. Devoting time and resources to learning and to cultivating connections to the broader research community can generate significant innovation advantages.

The recent developments in artificial intelligence (AI) have created business opportunities for the commercialization of technologies, which allow firms to speed up their learning and increase their absorptive capacity. An example of a firm operating in this space is BenchSci founded in 2015 and based in Toronto. Its first product, launched in 2017, is an AI software that uses advances in deep learning to read and interpret the latest scientific literature in biology. The main use of the technology is to help researchers working in pharmaceutical firms to identify the right antibodies required for the development of a new drug. This can substantially speed up the innovation process because the R&D personnel will have to spend less time surveying the relevant literature to identify the appropriate antibodies to use. Indeed, BenchSci has been very successful so far. By 2019, more than 3,600 research institutions and fifteen of the top twenty pharma companies used it. In total, more than 31,000 scientists have relied on BenchSci for their experiments.

## 6.8  Firm Size and Innovation

Are large firms more or less innovative than small firms? Extensive academic literature has examined this question and documented important differences in innovation activities across firms of different sizes.

A quick look at patent data indicates that large firms play a very important role in innovation. For example, in 2020 the five firms that applied for the most patents in the United States were all very large companies: IBM (9,130 patents), Samsung (6,415), Canon (3,225), Microsoft (2,905), and Intel (2,867). This simple measure of innovation activity clearly suggests that large firms are the most productive innovators.

In a comprehensive survey of the literature, Wesley Cohen describes several reasons why large firms may have an advantage in innovation.[25] First, it may be easier for large firms to raise the capital required to invest in risky R&D projects. Second, large firms may enjoy *economies of scope* in R&D. Economies of scope take place when an expense can be spread across a variety of different activities. For example, large firms can spread the costs of an expensive laboratory equipment over multiple research projects, and this cannot be done by a small startup working on a single research project. Third, the returns from R&D investments tend to be higher for firms with large sales volume. This is particularly the case for process innovation. For example, consider the possibility of developing a new manufacturing process that costs $100,000 and that can reduce the production costs of a product from $20 to $15. The new process will generate a cost saving of $5, which covers its development expense only if the firm sells more than 20,000 units. A firm with small market share, which does not expect to sell that amount, will not find the innovation investment profitable. Conversely, a large firm that expects to sell much more than 20,000 units will find the investment very attractive.

R&D investments also tend to be more productive in large firms thanks to their ability to own or access *complementary assets*.[26] These are resources or capabilities that are hard to develop or acquire and can generate an advantage in the product market. For example, it is easier for large medical device firms to commercialize a new product because of their existing relationships with hospitals and physicians and their brand names. Finally, large firms have an advantage in idea production due to within-firm knowledge spillovers. The insights from a research project in one unit of the firm may stimulate research activity in another unit of the firm.

On the other hand, research has also documented that a firm's size may also lead to disadvantages that reduce R&D productivity.

The most important one that has been noticed by the literature is the bureaucratic nature of many large corporations, which may slow down research activity. Despite this possibility, the empirical studies have shown a strong positive relationship between firm size, patenting, and the likelihood of performing R&D.

At the same time, management scholars have shown that differences in firm size are related not only to differences in the amount of innovation developed, but also to differences in the type of innovation activity performed. The key finding of this line of research is that large corporations are more likely to pursue relatively more incremental and more process innovation than smaller firms.[27] Small firms and new industry entrants are responsible for many radical innovations that disrupt specific industries. Research has shown how in the personal computer software industry new firms tend to create new software categories, while established firms tend to develop improvements in existing categories.[28]

One of the explanations for this finding is that the bureaucratization of large firms often leads them to only invest in innovations that "fit" with their established research activities and to overlook more radical projects.[29]

It is important for managers of large firms to be aware that firm size leads to a tendency to focus on incremental innovation. There are strategies that large firms can implement to generate stronger incentives to pursue more radical research projects. One example of such a strategy is Google's 20 percent time project. This strategy allows Google's employees to take 20 percent of their time out of their core jobs to work on projects of their choosing. In their 2004 Founders' IPO letter, Larry Page and Sergey Brin wrote:

*We encourage our employees, in addition to their regular projects, to spend 20% of their time working on what they think will most benefit Google. This empowers them to be more creative and innovative. Many of our significant advances have happened in this manner. For example, AdSense for content and Google News were both prototyped in "20% time."*[30]

In a sense, this strategy tries to create an entrepreneurial environment – that is, to generate many small firms – within the large company. Because small firms tend to have an advantage in generating more radical technologies, this can counterbalance the tendency of large corporations to focus on incremental innovation.

## 6.9 Competition and Innovation

Is there more innovation in industries where competition is intense or in industries where competition is soft? This question has received a lot of attention in the management and economics literature. It is important to ask this question because industry rivalry can change over time, for example with the beginning of a price war or with a big merger that consolidates the market supply. How do these changes in competition affect firm incentives to innovate?

A prominent study conducted by Philippe Aghion, Nicholas Bloom, Richard Blundell, Rachel Griffith, and Peter Howitt has examined this issue both theoretically and empirically. The key research finding is that there is an inverted-U relationship between innovation and competition.[31] At very low levels of competition, firms typically are not very innovative. The same appears to be true in industries where competition is very intense. According to the study, innovation appears to thrive at intermediate levels of competition.

Intuitively, when firms face limited industry competition, their incentives to innovate are low because consumers have limited options and the gains that a firm can make by offering superior products are limited. When competition is very intense, margins are thin. In this situation, firms may see innovation investments as too risky. If one R&D project fails, the loss generated may threaten the survival of the firm. Moreover, in a very competitive environment, the gains from successful innovation are more likely to be eroded by imitation or by alternative technologies developed by competitors. Thus, innovation incentives are highest when competitive pressure is intermediate. Managers feel the pressure, but it is not excessive.

The findings of Aghion and his coauthors imply that is not easy for managers or consultants to predict whether an increase in competition will lead to more or less technological innovation in an industry. It depends on whether the initial state of the industry is on the left or on the right of the peak of the inverted-U curve.

In the past two decades, many industries experienced a substantial increase in competitive pressure driven by a larger share of China's exports. In 1999, Chinese exports accounted for about 4 percent of global exports. By 2013, they accounted for almost 20 percent. An important driver for this surge was the reduction of trade barriers associated with China's accession to the World Trade Organization in 2001.[32]

Nicholas Bloom, Mirko Draca, and John Van Reenen provide a comprehensive analysis of how this change in the competition landscape affected the innovation investment of European firms.[33] Their analysis shows that Chinese competition led to an increase in innovation investments, which was driven by the European firms most affected by Chinese exports. A contemporaneous study performing a similar analysis for US firms found the opposite result. American firms responded to the rising Chinese competition by substantially reducing their innovation activity.[34]

The striking differences between what was observed in North America and Europe confirm the idea of the ambiguity of the effect of competition on innovation when the relationship is an inverted U. A variety of economic studies have shown that European markets tend to be less competitive than the American ones. The differential response therefore suggests that most European firms are located on the increasing part of the inverted U, and that most American firms are located on the decreasing part of the curve.

## 6.10 Technology S-curve

The technology S-curve is a popular tool used in economics and management to capture the relationship between the R&D investments aimed at improving a product or a process and the performance of the technology developed. It is called the S-curve because it has the shape of the letter S, as illustrated in Figure 6.1. It begins with a phase of slow improvements. The second step is a phase of fast acceleration in performance. The last part of the curve is a levelling-off associated with the maturity of the technology.

The technology S-curve has been shown to be a strong empirical regularity across technologies, industries, and countries. As explained in a classic book by Richard Foster, in most technology areas progress tends to be slow when initial investments are made to develop a new product or process. This initial phase typically continues until researchers reach a breakthrough that leads to fast improvement in performance. Eventually, it becomes more and

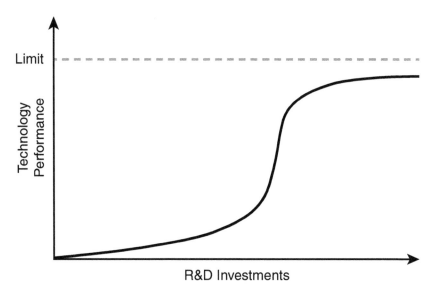

**Figure 6.1.** The technology S curve

more difficult to improve the performance of the technology and returns to R&D investments become more modest.[35]

It is important for managers to have a sense of the stage within the S-curve for the main technologies in their firms. Sometime, consultants generate actual estimates of S-curves. As Foster describes, this is typically done in three steps. The first is to assess the current stage in the S-curve. This requires an examination of the history of product introductions and an assessment of the improvements in performance across the various generations of the technology. One also needs information on the R&D effort that went into developing that product. The second step is to identify the performance limit, that is, the top of the S-curve. This requires an understanding of the laws of physics and the engineering constraints, which are expected to eventually bind. The final step involves projection of the historical performance into the future. This is often done with computer programs and econometric software that extrapolate the S-curve from the available data.

For managers who do not have the time or the resources to empirically estimate S-curves, the key issue is to understand whether or not a technology has reached its limits. If the technical limits have already been reached, further innovation will be hard, no matter how much a firm tries. In this case, it is unlikely that a firm can create business value through additional R&D investments in the technology. It is probably more effective to invest the resources in other activities, such as marketing or purchasing. When technologies reach their maturity, it is also easier for competitors to catch up to the market leaders. More importantly at this stage, new S-curves may emerge, as I discuss in the next section.

## 6.11 Disruptive Innovation

Often, as one technology reaches its maturity, firms attempt to address an underlying consumer need using novel technological

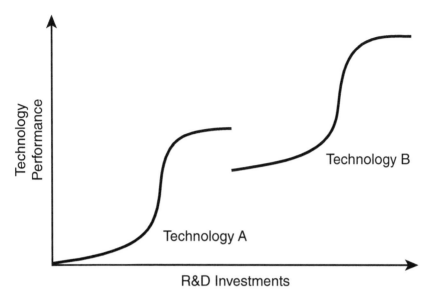

**Figure 6.2.** Disruption

approaches. Most of these attempts typically fail, but sometimes they succeed and translate into something significant.

This implies that, at any given time, many technological S-curves can exist. In most cases, new S-curves emerge but lie substantially below the current dominant technology. But if one of them reaches performance levels that are superior to the more mature technology, a new dominant technology may emerge. In this case, we say that the new S-curve generated a *technology disruption*. This is illustrated in Figure 6.2.

The idea of disruptive innovation was developed by Clay Christensen in an influential book titled *The Innovator's Dilemma*. Christensen wanted to understand why successful companies fail. His main finding was that in many cases failure arises because firms continue on the path that made them successful in the first place.[36]

According to Christensen to generate disruption, a technology should possess three characteristics. First, it should underperform compared to established firm's products in serving the needs of mainstream consumers. Second, it should be attractive for a niche segment of consumers that is underserved by established firms. Third, the technology should rapidly improve along the dimensions that mainstream consumers care about.

The idea is that a small group of consumers creates an entry opportunity for a new product that initially performs worse on some dimensions but rapidly improves on others. As the quality of the new product increases, the competitive pressure faced by the incumbents increases. Moreover, when the improvement in the new products is fast enough, incumbents may find themselves unable to respond effectively until it is too late.

A classic example of disruption, described in detail in the book *The Disruption Dilemma* by Joshua Gans, is what happened to *Encyclopedia Britannica*. In 1985, Microsoft, a young startup at the time, approached Encyclopedia Britannica (the leading encyclopedia company) with the idea to partner and commercialize a digital encyclopedia in CD-ROM format. Britannica turned the proposal down. This was not a surprising outcome; computers were in few households at that time.[37]

Moreover, an important driver of consumers' value of encyclopedias was the ability to display the books, which was typically interpreted as an investment in your children's future. The sales pitch of Britannica was that for about $1,000 you could invest substantially in the education of your children. Britannica underestimated the fact that the PC market improved dramatically in the late '80s and early '90s. And during the 1990s it was possible to spend $1,000 to get a PC that fulfilled the same dreams as Britannica and included Encarta, a relatively cheap encyclopedia offered by Microsoft.

There are various ways in which an established firm operating on a mature technology may respond to the threat of disruption. Research by Joshua Gans identifies four possible strategies. The first is to create new independent ventures that invest heavily in potentially disruptive technologies. The second is to integrate the new technology by developing innovation along multiple research paths. The third is to aggressively invest in a new technology as it reaches the performance levels of the more mature technology.[38]

The final strategy is to cooperate or acquire disruptive new entrants. In some industries, such as life sciences and high tech, this strategy may lead to "killer acquisitions." In such acquisitions, large firms intend to discontinue the startup's innovation projects and preempt future competition. Colleen Cunningham, Florian Ederer, and Song Ma provide a detailed analysis of the phenomenon in the pharmaceutical industry, showing that many acquired drug projects are not developed by acquiring firms even if they overlap with the acquirer's existing product portfolio. These acquisitions are the center of several academic and policy debates because they pose concerns for consumer welfare.[39]

# CHAPTER 7

# Innovation Ecosystems

*Access to talented and creative people is to modern business what access to coal and iron ore was to steel-making.*

– Richard Florida[1]

## 7.1 Eight Factors That Drive Regional Innovation

In Chapter 6, I examined how the innovation activity of a firm may be shaped by internal factors (such as corporate culture or compensation schemes) and by factors related to the industry in which the firm operates (such as competitive pressure).

The location of a firm also has profound effects on its innovation. Some places are characterized by particularly strong innovation performance. Software and ICT companies, such as Apple, Google, and Facebook, have flourished in what is called the Silicon Valley region of the San Francisco Bay area. Microsoft and Amazon have thrived in Seattle. Boston and New York are two other prominent US technology centers. From a global perspective, leading innovation hubs include London, Toronto, Tel-Aviv, Singapore, Shanghai, and Bangalore.

The key role played by firms' locations has been documented by a large number of studies spanning diverse academic disciplines,

| | |
|---|---|
| Investors | Competitors |
| Consumers | Institutions |
| Suppliers | Culture |
| Labor pool | Social network |

**Figure 7.1.** Factors shaping regional technological innovation

including economics, management, political science, sociology, and geography. In a chapter of the book *Survive and Thrive*, Ajay Agrawal and I provide a survey of this body of research.[2] Our analysis suggests that the regional characteristics that appear to have the largest impact on innovation can be classified into the following eight categories: investors, consumers, suppliers, labor pool, competitors, institutions, culture, and social network.

These eight factors – illustrated in Figure 7.1 – shape the innovation activity of a geographical region through multiple channels. First, they influence the entry of new high-tech firms by creating conditions that affect their growth. Second, they affect the innovation productivity and the technology adoption strategies of large firms. Third, they shape the interaction between firms of different sizes.

This chapter examines each of these forces and discusses how they can affect firms' technology strategies. It is important to notice that these forces complement each other. Technological innovation tends to flourish in locations where several of these factors are present.

## 7.2 Investors

The first factor identified in the eight-factor framework relates to access to capital. Financing is a key requirement for business success, and it is particularly important for high-tech entrepreneurs who are often cash constrained and may require substantial resources to develop, test, and commercialize their technologies.

In general, various options are available to technology startups looking to raise the funds required for their business activity. Capital can be internal (self-financing) or can be obtained from external sources. A report of the Kauffman Foundation shows that many new businesses rely heavily on personal savings and self-financing.[3] While self-financing is common in many industries, it is not a feasible option for many science-based startups, which require substantial resources to translate scientific research into a revenue-generating business. The pharmaceutical industry is an example of a setting in which relying on self-financing is impossible, because the required financial resources are very large. Estimates suggest that the average cost for the development of a new drug is about $1.4 billion, and the average time from the start of clinical testing to sales is close to 100 months. It is extremely unlikely that the founders of a new firm can afford such expenditure without external financing.[4]

There are two main types of external financing: debt and equity. Debt is funds borrowed from other parties, which require interest payments. Equity grants the investor ownership in the company. Two sources of external capital are extremely common among high-tech startups: angel and venture capital (VC) investors. Angels are professional investors who use their personal funds to obtain equity stakes in early-stage ventures. VCs are firms that invest large amounts of money in portfolios of startup ventures. VCs typically raise their capital from large institutions, such as pension funds and insurance companies, which are interested in high-risk/high-return opportunities. VC financing takes place in rounds: Series A, followed by a Series B, a Series C, and so on. This process typically continues until the venture is acquired by another firm, or it goes public through an initial public offering (IPO) on a stock exchange.

The presence of many VCs and angel investors in a region can be very beneficial for technology startups, because investors vary in their willingness to operate in certain technology areas and in their knowledge of specific sectors. For example, in Toronto, the venture capital firm Radical Ventures specializes in artificial intelligence whereas the firm Lumira Ventures specializes in healthcare and life sciences. Even within a specific sector, firms may differ substantially in their risk tolerance and in the composition of investment portfolios. This implies that it is not easy for startups to find VCs with liquid funds and willingness to invest in their technologies. In fact, rejection is the most common outcome when entrepreneurs pitch their business ideas to investors. For these reasons, a thick supply of angels and VCs in a region can significantly enhance the likelihood that a technology startup raises capital.

Numerous empirical studies have shown that the geographical location of VCs is extremely concentrated. This is especially the case in North America, where the vast majority of VC offices are based in three regions: Silicon Valley, Boston, and New York. According to a study by Henry Chen, Paul Gompers, Anna Kovner, and Josh Lerner, these locations account for roughly 10 percent of US entrepreneurship but for about 60 percent of US venture capital. Such geographical concentration far exceeds concentrations observed in other economic sectors.[5]

The high spatial concentration of VCs has important implications for the location strategy of technology entrepreneurs, because VCs are more likely to invest and serve on boards of local companies. The negative impact of the geographic distance between a VC and a startup has been documented by several studies in economics and finance. For example, Shai Bernstein, Xavier Giroud, and Richard Townsend examine the effects of the introduction of a new direct airline route on the behavior of VCs and firms in locations connected by the route. The study argues that, once a new route is opened, VCs tend to become more involved with companies located at the new destination because VC investors are more likely to visit companies in their portfolio if they can be reached with a direct flight. Greater involvement of VC investors leads to better relationships with management teams and to a better understanding of the challenges faced by the portfolio companies. Indeed, Bernstein and coauthors show that VC-founded companies become more innovative and are more likely to have a successful exit (via IPO or acquisition) following the introduction of a direct flight.[6]

Overall, the literature has emphasized that investors in new technologies – especially angels and VCs – do not simply provide funds to companies. They also generate value through other activities that require geographical proximity. These activities include mentorship and connections to suppliers and buyers.

## 7.3 Consumers

Most new firms begin their business activity by selling locally; they expand to national and international markets only after their products show success in their markets of origin. For example, Starbucks operated various coffee stores in Seattle before expanding to Vancouver and Chicago. Similarly, Walmart opened several stores in Arkansas before expanding to Missouri and Oklahoma. In this respect, the growth of new companies can be strongly affected by the level and quality of the local demand.

The idea that the size of the market served by a firm can have substantial effects on its innovation and productivity goes back to Adam Smith who, in the book *The Wealth of Nations*, postulated that "the division of labor is limited by the extent of the market."[7] Smith's intuition was that a large market demand can lead to cost savings by allowing firms to spread their fixed costs over a large customer base. This is particularly important for firms requiring investment in specialized equipment or labor-force training, because those expenditures would not be profitable if the market were too small. From this perspective, high-tech firms that can leverage a large local demand may have an advantage in terms of cost-spreading and innovation potential.

Startup companies often learn new aspects of their technology and develop ideas on how to fine-tune their products by interacting with their customers. Product development partnerships are especially common when the early customers of a startup are large corporate buyers.[8]

A context where customers represent an important source of technical knowledge is the medical device industry. Practicing doctors can provide important insights on unmet needs and on potential opportunities for device improvements. Medical professionals may even contribute directly to the innovation process by inventing themselves. A famous example of a physician innovator is Dr. Thomas Fogarty, the inventor of the Fogarty catheter. Fogarty discovered a new type of balloon catheter, which substantially increased the chances of survival for patients requiring removal of blood clots. He patented the device and licensed it to Edwards Life Sciences. He then continued to practice medicine, and became a well-known serial inventor, with over 70 patents.[9]

Research by Ronnie Chatterji, Kira Fabrizio, Will Mitchell, and Kevin Schulman shows that the contribution of physicians to medical device innovation is widespread in the US. According to their analysis, practicing doctors accounted for almost 20 percent of the medical device patents filed in the US during 1990–6. In most cases, physician innovators do not start new companies because they lack the business knowledge required to manufacture and commercialize a new medical device. Instead, they license their invention to medical device companies and collaborate with their licensees, which provide the expertise required for the development of the product.[10]

Medical devices developed by practicing physicians are an example of *user innovation*. Users are economic agents who benefit from a technology by using it. They differ from manufacturers, which expect to benefit by selling their technologies. This distinction has been emphasized by Eric von Hippel, who documents how user innovations play important roles in various industries. An important insight from von Hippel's research is that companies can be more innovative if they interact with their lead users, that is, their more creative customers who may come up with new variants of existing products.[11]

## 7.4  Suppliers

In comparing California's Silicon Valley with Boston's Route 128, Anna Lee Saxenian reports the following insight from a Silicon Valley entrepreneur:

> It's hard for a small company to start in Route 128 because you can't get stuff like ICs and disk drives fast. Route 128 is dominated by large, vertically integrated firms that do everything themselves. In Silicon Valley, you can get anything you want on the market. You can get all those things in Route 128 sooner or later, but the decisions are much faster if you're in Silicon Valley.[12]

As suggested by this quote, being located in a region with many suppliers can provide multiple benefits. First, transportation costs and waiting times for inputs will be lower. Fast access to input was one of the crucial factors that led Jeff Bezos to locate Amazon in Seattle, which was near Ingram Books, the largest distributor of books in the country. Second, as in the case of customers, suppliers may become strategic partners in technology development. More broadly, interactions with suppliers may be a powerful source of new product ideas because firms can identify new materials and components to test. Indeed, a large survey of US manufacturing firms shows that interactions with suppliers is one of the most important sources of corporate inventions.[13]

The presence of multiple suppliers in one area may also increase the bargaining power of local firms. Intuitively, ventures can increase their profits when they have the opportunity to shop around for the best prices, input quality, and product fit. In a detailed empirical analysis of new firms' location strategies, Juan Alcácer and Wilbur Chung provide support to this idea, showing that new entrants tend to avoid locations where inputs are sold by only very few suppliers.[14]

In some industries, ventures have little choice as to their location because the economic activity may be naturally constrained to specific regions. For instance, desert areas are often inadequate for agriculture, whereas coastal regions are preferable for ship building. Office spaces are also key inputs for new ventures. The housing stock, office vacancies, rents, and other features of the regional real-estate market should be carefully assessed when developing a startup location strategy.

## 7.5 Labor Pools

In choosing their location, high-tech firms must pay close attention to the local labor supply. As suggested by Richard Florida in the epigraph to this chapter, they especially need to carefully assess whether workers specialized in the relevant technology fields are present in the region or can be attracted to the region. The larger the labor pool, the easier it will be for the firm to find the best match for their needs.

Another reason why large pools of highly skilled workers can be an engine of technology entrepreneurship is that circulation of ideas among them may lead to the discovery of entrepreneurial opportunities. Alfred Marshall was one of the first economists to point this out, as he wrote:

> *If one man starts a new idea, it is taken up by others and combined with suggestions of their own; and thus it becomes the source of further new ideas.*[15]

Economists Enrico Berkes and Ruben Gaetani provide empirical evidence showing that locations with a high density of specialized labor have an advantage in developing "unconventional innovations." These are innovations that combine technology categories that are rarely seen together. Development of these technologies requires a greater diversity of contributors, and the products that embed them often have a disruptive economic impact.[16]

In considering labor pools, managers should focus not only on the technical knowledge of the workforce but also on the business knowledge and work experience of the talent in the region. One of Silicon Valley's greatest advantages relative to other locations is that this region has a disproportionately large labor force with experience in scaling startups. These are managers who oversaw a user base going from zero to millions of users, who raised large equity capital investments, and who recruited large numbers of engineers and software developers. These are skills that cannot be easily learned in business school; rather, they are gained through learning-by-doing.[17]

Several strands of research have documented how specialized workers tend to agglomerate in a limited number of regions. The presence of research institutes, universities, and hospitals is often a crucial determinant of the presence of large labor pools. Universities, in particular, have been shown to be important drivers of local economic growth. There are various channels through which this effect takes place. First, universities educate and train new generations of specialized workers, so their undergraduate and graduate programs are key drivers of labor pool formation. Second, research-oriented universities tend to attract specialized workers to the area who plan to collaborate or interact with university researchers. Third, universities and research hospitals are important generators of new ideas and technologies that are often shared with and further developed by local businesses.[18]

## 7.6 Competition

It is important for managers of high-tech firms to have a good understanding of their local competitive landscape, with special attention to large corporations and startup firms active in their region. Local competitive pressure has its costs and its benefits. On the one hand, firms may profit from a low level of regional competition, as summarized by the following quote by venture capitalist Jeremy Levine:

> There are some great advantages in building a company where no one else goes [because] the founders have unbounded enthusiasm; they enjoy a virtual monopoly on technical talent, and they can attract incredible loyalty from employees.[19]

At the same time, as I examined in Chapter 6, the economics literature has shown that competition can play an important role in disciplining managers and spurring innovation.

Identifying the key competitors a firm faces in a regional environment is not an easy task. A common managerial mistake is to have a narrow focus and to consider only firms with products or technologies very similar to those of the focal firm. At the local level, firms compete not only in the product market but also for inputs, talent, and funding. Therefore, it is important to identify the relevant regional "cluster" of interconnected firms producing related products. Special attention must be paid to large companies present in the area, which often act as "anchor tenants" in the regional innovation system. These large companies can have a profound impact on the regional economy by stimulating the demand for new technology from startup companies and by attracting a skilled labor to the area.[20]

Several management studies have shown that employees of large companies come up with many ideas for new products and processes that are often turned down because their employers decide to commercialize only new technologies that have high fit with their established research trajectories. For example, in 2001 only five out of more than 2,000 new product proposals by General Electric employees were accepted for product development.[21] In several of these cases, the innovator left their employer and commercialized the "misfit" inventions through the formation of what is called a "spinout" venture.

The urban economics literature has shown that spinouts are common in geographic areas where many small firms are already active. This is because the existence of a sizable mass of small firms thickens the local markets for ancillary services, and this reduces the costs of setting up a new firm.[22] Examples of these industry-specific ancillary services include early-stage capital (specialized angel investors and VCs) as well as specialized real estate and legal services. Moreover, the presence of small firms in a geographic area may create a culture of entrepreneurship that itself stimulates additional entry of new firms.[23]

These considerations suggest that large corporations and small high-tech firms are complementary forces shaping the level of innovation in a region. Large firms have high innovation propensity and drive the regional technological activity by developing new technologies directly or through their spinouts. At the same time, the presence of a large pool of small firms magnifies this effect by lowering the cost of entry for new firms and spinouts. In other words, the innovative potential of a region is maximized when many small firms and several large firms coexist.

My research with Ajay Agrawal, Iain Cockburn, and Alexander Oettl conducts an empirical analysis of the US regional innovation systems and provides support to the idea that the development of new technologies is higher in regions in which several large corporate labs and a large number of small high-tech firms coexist. Specifically, our study finds that these regions experience a 17 percent increase in innovation relative to geographic areas in which firm size diversity is not present.[24]

## 7.7 Institutions

Adam Smith was one of the first scholars to notice that "order and good government, and along with them the liberty and security of individuals" are important for the success of a business activity.[25] Well-functioning public institutions, such as courts, healthcare providers, and law enforcement, are key determinants of national and regional economic growth. These aspects are particularly important for companies considering international locations, because institutional differences across countries can be substantially larger than those across regions within countries.

A study by Michael Seitz and Martin Watzinger shows that international differences in the quality of legal systems, and particularly in firms' ability to enforce business contracts, can have important effects on R&D investments. This is because firms are typically less willing to invest in the development of new products or in the adoption of new technologies if there is uncertainty about the capacity of the judicial system to enforce contracts with suppliers and customers. Similarly, uncertainty in the effectiveness of IP protection can also discourage R&D investments. Their analysis shows that this effect is large. According to their computations, about one-quarter of the gap in R&D between Italian and German car producers are due to differences in the "rule of law."[26]

Backlogs in regional courts, regional business legislation, and local taxation levels can substantially affect the profits of a firm and its ability to attract talent. Ufuk Akcigit, Salomé Baslandze, and Stefanie Stantcheva show that superstar inventors' location choices are significantly affected by the tax rates.[27] In research conducted with Mark Schankerman and Carlos Serrano, we show that local taxes strongly affect patent transactions as well.[28]

Transport infrastructures, such as airports, train stations, and roads, also have important effects on firms' ability to interact with consumers, suppliers, investors, and competitors. An article I coauthored with Ajay Agrawal and Alexander Oettl shows that transport infrastructures facilitate the local circulation of knowledge. In particular, we show that in regions where the stock of transportation infrastructure is larger, innovators are more likely to build on technologies developed by firms geographically more distant.[29]

## 7.8 Culture

Anna Lee Saxenian emphasized that differences in local culture can translate into differences in entrepreneurship activity. In particular, she noticed how in Silicon Valley there is a unique forgiving attitude toward entrepreneurs who failed in previous ventures, which facilitates the creation of new firms.[30]

The cultural norms of different locations can have important effects on innovation activity. Knowledge flows are shaped by the interaction between different demographic and ethnic groups within a region. The greater the diversity of people exchanging ideas, the more likely it is that innovation will thrive. Research has shown that regional amenities, such as restaurants, museums, stadiums, and concert halls, play important roles into attracting diverse talent.

Tolerance toward different lifestyle types (families, singles, ethnic diversity, age diversity, LGBTQ+, etc.) is also an important factor that attracts key talent in the region.

Having a diverse population residing in a region does not guarantee that a diverse pool of inventors actually participates in the innovation process. Indeed, the empirical evidence suggests a lack of diversity in technological innovation even in countries and regions characterized by substantial ethnic and gender diversity. For example, estimates indicate that men receive about 87 percent of all US patents.[31]

In the medical sciences, research publications by mixed-gender teams have been shown to be substantially more novel and impactful than the publications by same-gender teams of equivalent size.[32] Rembrand Koning, Sampsa Samila, and John-Paul Ferguson conduct a detailed textual analysis of all US biomedical patents filed between 1976 and 2010 and show that female inventors are more likely to work on women's health and to develop biomedical technologies that focus on the needs of women.[33] This result has important implications because it suggests that gender imbalances in the innovation process may affect the direction of technological progress. In the specific context of medical technologies, the study suggests that shortages of projects, procedures, and products aimed at female patients may be due to gender imbalances in the innovation process.

A study by Alex Bell, Raj Chetty, Xavier Jaravel, Neviana Petkova, and John Van Reenen examines US innovation activity and shows that children's chances of becoming inventors vary sharply with the characteristics of the social environment in which they grow up. The main finding of this study is that exposure to innovation during childhood has a very large impact on children's propensities to become an innovator. Children who grow up with a patentee as family member, or in a neighborhood where many patentees live, are much more likely to become patentees themselves. A very important implication of this research is that the superior innovation rates of some geographical areas tend to be long lasting, because the propensity to be highly innovative is transferred across generations.[34]

## 7.9 Social Network

Each person is embedded in multiple networks of social relations generated by their family, friends, and civic connections. The "social capital" derived from the personal relationships of workers and managers can be used by firms in multiple ways. Technology entrepreneurs, in particular, can leverage their connections to raise capital and to find customers, suppliers, and employees.

It is not necessarily better to move to an innovation hub, such as Silicon Valley, when entrepreneurs or managers have a deep social network in their home locations. As in the famous quote from *Julius Caesar*, in some cases it may be preferable to be *"first in a village than second in Rome."*[35] Moreover, locations in which newcomers are welcome and can easily form social connections are more attractive than locations where integration is challenging.

The entrepreneurship literature has shown that immigration flows are an important determinant of the level of technological entrepreneurship in a region, because immigrants have higher entrepreneurship rates than natives.[36] Building on this finding, research by Astrid Marinoni shows that the presence of enclaves (high share of conationals) reduces the difference in entrepreneurship rates between immigrants and natives; it also increases the average quality of the firms established by immigrants. Marinoni's findings are consistent with the idea that immigrants face higher barriers to entry into local labor markets relative to natives. These barriers induce immigrants to become entrepreneurs because it is challenging for them to find jobs in local companies. The social ties generated by the presence of a large group of conationals facilitate access to wage employment, which in turn reduces the level of necessity-based entrepreneurship.[37]

## 7.10  Linking Location Strategy with Technology Strategy

Multidisciplinary research on innovation ecosystems has shown that the eight factors discussed in this chapter are key determinants of a thriving regional environment. Ignoring them may lead startup founders and corporate managers to pick the wrong location for their businesses.

Overall, the framework that I developed with Ajay Agrawal suggests that the way a regional ecosystem affects innovation may differ across firms because it depends on the technological needs of the company and on how important each factor is for its business model.

Even for a specific firm, whether an innovation ecosystem is a good fit or not can change over time. For example, several startup ventures that moved to Silicon Valley decided to return to their home location at a certain stage. This was the case for the Canadian A/B testing startup Taplytics, which moved from Toronto to Silicon Valley because of its investors and customers. But, as time passed, Taplytics's products started getting traction with a number of prominent corporate clients located outside California, and this led the firm to relocate to Toronto, where the firm was able to enjoy lower tax rates and a sizable talent pool.

The eight-factor analysis is also useful in shaping the location decision of large technology companies because their innovation performance may be strongly affected by the presence of high-tech startups in the region. Large firms thrive in regions with high-tech entrepreneurship because they are often well positioned to license technologies developed by smaller firms that may not have the manufacturing and commercialization capabilities required to take new products to the market. Technology startups can also be an important source of talent for large companies. Take, for example, the move of General Electric (GE) headquarters from Connecticut to Boston in 2016. In a statement explaining the relocation, GE's CEO Jeffet Immelt described Boston's startup environment as "an ecosystem that shares our aspirations."[38]

There is an important difference in the way the regional environment affects the innovation activity of large and small firms. Small firms do not have the resources to substantially change the ecosystem in which they are located; they may simply decide whether to stay or to leave for a new location. Conversely, large firms may have the resources and the bargaining power required to shape their ecosystem. Take, for example, regional labor pools. A small startup can tap on the local supply of talent by hiring graduates from local universities. There is little a small company can do if the workforce of the region does not have some of the skills required by the firm. A large company may instead engage in initiatives that can shape the local supply of talent. For example, it may enter a strategic partnership with a local university, providing resources to develop research centers or graduate programs related to specific technology areas.

# CHAPTER 8

# Health, Safety, and Innovation

*Never let a good crisis go to waste.*

– Winston Churchill[1]

## 8.1 Product Safety and Technology Strategy

Since 2014, General Motors (GM) recalled more than 2.6 million cars because of defective ignition switches linked to 125 deaths and 275 injuries. GM had to pay more than $2.6 billion in penalties and settlements for this technology failure.

Catastrophic accidents like this may have profound impacts on a firm and may even threaten its very existence. It is not surprising that in this type of situation, many firms replace their executives and substantially rethink their business strategy. In the case of GM, a statement was released in which the company affirmed that it "took the lessons it learned from the ignition switch recalls and has transformed its culture to focus on customer safety,"[2] which resonates with the epigraph by Winston Churchill.

Health and safety concerns are of first-order importance in many aspects of our lives. Yet, firms often articulate technology strategies that pay only limited attention to technological failures and their impact on the health and safety of consumers. Over-looking these aspects can be extremely costly, both socially and privately. To begin with, product liability litigation is widespread, accounting for the majority of civil personal injury cases in the United States. On top of the large monetary costs associated with litigation, product failures tend to attract media coverage and public attention. Take, for example, the fatal accident in March 2018 involving Uber's autonomous vehicle; consider also the Boeing 737 MAX crashes in Indonesia and Ethiopia. Such media spotlights can have profound impacts on the safety perceived by consumers, and on the overall reputation of the firm involved.

It is natural for entrepreneurs, corporate managers, engineers, and scientists to be excited about their discoveries. Questions like "Will consumers like this new feature?" and "How much will they be willing to pay for it?" often dominate the discussions related to the commercialization of new products. But this may lead management to focus on the best-case scenarios, in which the new technologies work perfectly. In this chapter, I will discuss how this can be a problem and examine how product failures and their impact on users can shape firms' technology strategies.

## 8.2 Product Safety Regulation

Countries all over the world regulate product safety through a variety of laws and codes. In the United States, the Consumer Product Safety Commission (CPSC) is the main agency with authority over safety regulation and recalls for consumer products. Safety of cars, trucks, and motorcycles is overseen by the Department of Transportation. Risks associated with food, drugs, and cosmetics are instead assessed by the Food and Drug Administration.

In Canada, the safety of consumer products is regulated by the Canada Consumer Product Safety Act (CPSA), which prohibits firms from importing, manufacturing, and selling products that are dangerous for human health or safety. This law also requires firms to retain documentation that allows for the tracing of consumer products through the supply chain and gives authority to Health Canada to recall dangerous products. In Europe, safety requirements for general consumer products are regulated by the General Product Safety Directive.

In practice, most of the safety regulation takes place through voluntary standards that are developed by the firms operating in a particular sector through standard development organizations. Mandatory standards are standards that have been incorporated into a law and thus require compliance. Many voluntary standards are "incorporated by reference" into the law, which essentially makes them mandatory.

For some products, safety is regulated through special legislation. Two of the most regulated sectors in this respect are drugs and medical devices. To commercialize a new drug or a new medical device in the United States, companies must receive approval from the Food and Drug Administration (FDA). In the case of drugs, the first step for a firm with sufficient pre-clinical data is to submit an Investigational New Drug (IND) application. Once the FDA has reviewed the IND application, clinical trials are conducted in three phases. *Phase I* centers around safety. It typically involves twenty to eighty healthy volunteers and aims to identify side effects and establish safe dose ranges. *Phase II* emphasizes effectiveness. The drug is tested in several hundred people with a specific disease or condition and its effects are compared to those of a placebo administered to a control group. Finally, in *Phase III*, effectiveness and safety are assessed in large-scale trials involving often more than thousand patients.

If the outcomes of these three clinical trials are successful, the firm can submit a New Drug Application (NDA) to the FDA. The FDA reviews the information on the NDA (from trials, pre-clinical studies, and labeling) and provides final approval for the drug. Once the drug has been approved and marketed, there is still post-marketing monitoring by the FDA, which may include additional trials (*Phase IV*).

Medical devices are classified by the FDA into one of three groups depending on their risk and intended use. *Class I* devices, such as an elastic bandage, carry the lowest risk. *Class II* are devices like electric wheelchairs, which have some potential for harm. *Class III* devices, such as pacemakers, are those carrying the highest risk. Class III devices are often implanted in the human body and are life supporting.

Most of the medical devices in Class I are exempted from FDA approval. To market some of the Class I devices and most Class II devices, firms need to submit a pre-market notification, also known as a 510(k) application. In a 510(k) application, a firm explains that its device is a modification of an existing device. Specifically, one needs to show that the new device is as safe as a similar device already on the market and that the underlying core technology is substantially equivalent. A few Class II devices and all Class III devices require pre-market approval, also called PMA application. Extensive pre-clinical and clinical data is needed to obtain approval via PMA.

The long and complex approval process for pharmaceuticals and medical devices is based on an important public policy trade-off. On the one hand, the clinical trials create value by screening unsafe products and decreasing uncertainty about their health effectiveness. On the other hand, the process has the potential cost of reducing the products available on the market because of delayed commercialization and higher entry costs due to testing.

This trade-off was heavily discussed in the press as vaccines for COVID-19 were developed and tested. Take, for example, the vaccine developed in a collaboration between Oxford University and the pharmaceutical firm AstraZeneca. Trials began in April 2020, less than four months after the team of scientists led by Professor Sarah Gilbert and Professor Andrew Pollard began to work to create a COVID-19 vaccine. But approval from the UK regulatory agency was only obtained at the end of December 2020 and the first doses of vaccine rolled out in the UK on the fourth of January 2021. Advocates of shorter trials argued that reducing the length of the clinical trials would have permitted a faster deployment of the vaccine. At the same time, concerns were raised that faster approval had to come at the cost of greater uncertainty on the safety and efficacy of the product.

Economists Matthew Grennan and Robert Town present a detailed examination of this trade-off generated by regulatory screening.[3] They compare the European and the US medical device approval process and document a substantial difference in the amount of pre-market testing required from manufacturers in the two countries. For Class III devices in particular, the EU screening is faster and less costly than the one in the US. As a result, EU consumers enjoy greater access to the newest medical devices. According to Grennan and Town, 23 percent of the heart stents used in the EU are never commercialized in the United States and, when they are commercialized, EU physicians have access to them ten months earlier than their US counterparts. At the same time, Grennan and Town show that EU consumers face greater uncertainty about the safety and effectiveness of the technologies, because EU regulation allows entry of devices with less evidence on product efficacy.

The pharmaceutical regulatory process has also been shown to have important effects on innovation activity. The large capital required to go through the three phases of the FDA clinical trials provides an advantage for big pharmaceutical companies, which are not financially constrained. Moreover, the time required to conduct the clinical trials reduces the period in which sales can take place under patent protection. This occurs because pharmaceutical firms typically file for patents at the time of the scientific discovery and long clinical trials generate a substantial lag between discovery and product sales. This reduces the effective length of the patent. Eric Budish, Benjamin Roin, and Heidi Williams show that this is a problem for certain areas of cancer research. The length of clinical trials varies substantially across cancer drugs. For example, it takes about three years to conduct clinical trials for metastatic prostate cancer drugs and eighteen years for localized prostate cancer trials. Exploiting this variation, the study shows that when clinical trials are very long, private companies are less likely to invest in drug discovery because the useful patent life (the years of sales which will be protected by a twenty-year patent) is shorter.[4]

## 8.3  Product Liability Risk

To sell their products in a country, firms are required to comply with its national safety standards and regulations. Even when the products comply with these basic safety norms, firms may still be liable for harms and injuries generated by their products. For example, medical devices and pharmaceutical firms are often the target of product liability lawsuits after their products successfully pass the FDA screening process.[5]

In the United States, product liability litigation cases typically involve an assessment of whether one of three types of product defects existed at the time a product was sold. The first is *manufacturing defects*. This relates to products that are not manufactured or assembled as intended. A classic example of manufacturing defect is food containing a hazard that consumers do not reasonably expect, such as a dead mouse inside a soft drink can. Other examples include a bed incorrectly assembled in a factory, or a drug contaminated at a processing facility that ends up harming the final consumer.

The second type of defects is *warning defects*. These relate to risks of harm that could have been reduced if additional instructions or warnings were provided. Examples include labels that do not specify that a product has a hot surface that may cause burns. In the case of food, not disclosing allergenic effects of the product is often considered a warning defect.

The final type of defects is *design defects*, which relate to flaws in product design that injure users or other persons. Consider, for example, an incorrectly designed mobile phone battery that generates excessive heat and results in fire. Design defect litigation is the most prevalent form of liability litigation. For example, design defects have been the leading cause of US toy recalls during the past thirty years. Toy design flaws include sharp edges, long strings, and small detachable parts.[6]

Design litigation involves substantial uncertainty because courts must consider in what alternative ways a product could have been designed, and what would have happened if this had been the case. In principle, a firm can sell a product that is as safe as all other products in the market and still be at fault if a feasible design alternative could have prevented an accident. To deal with these challenges, many technology firms engage in "defensive design," that is, product design that tries to anticipate product liability issues simulating fault-modes and worst-case scenarios.[7]

One of the most famous historical cases of design defect involved the Ford Pinto, a very popular automobile sold in the United States in the late 1960s and in the 1970s. In 1968, when Ford's president Lee Iaccoca decided to launch the Pinto, the company advertised the car as a vehicle that did "not weigh an ounce over 2,000 pounds" and did "not cost a penny over $2,000."[8] A key design feature of the car was that the fuel tank was placed behind the rear axle and in front of the rear bumper. This created serious problems because the tank would easily rupture and leak fuel during a rear-end collision.

In 1972, in a tragic accident, a Pinto was hit from behind and burst into flame. This received massive media coverage. An article in the magazine *Mother Jones* described the Pinto as a "firetrap" and alleged that Ford knew about the defect and did not want to redesign the car because it was not profitable.[9]

In 1978, all Ford Pintos were recalled and upgraded without charges to the owners. In particular, cars were modified by adding longer filler pipes and plastic shields to protect the tank. But this was not enough to protect Ford from a public relations disaster. Consumer perception about the safety of the Pinto, as well as of other Ford models, led to a decline in market demand and to a substantial drop in Ford's market share. Eventually, the Pinto was discontinued in 1980.

## 8.4  Risk-Mitigating Technologies

Risk-mitigating technologies (RMTs) are innovations that reduce the probability of negative events or the severity of their consequences. Windshield wipers, for example, reduce the likelihood of automobile accidents. Seat belts and airbags mitigate the negative effects of car crashes. RMTs may take various forms, depending on the nature of the hazards, the preferences of the consumers, and the technological possibilities. They can be incremental innovations that refine existing technologies or radical innovations that potentially establish entirely new classes of products.[10]

In Chapter 6, I examined the distinction between product and process innovation. The former includes technologies that improve existing products; the latter relates to improvements in manufacturing processes. RMTs may involve new types of products and of production processes. Assembly-line modifications that more effectively identify manufacturing defects, or the use of checklists during surgeries to reduce medical errors, are examples of RMTs related to process innovation.

On closer examination, one can notice that new, safer products inherently possess features both of product innovation and of process innovation. This is an important difference between RMTs and more traditional technological improvements that increase other quality aspects of a product. To show this, we need to extend the formula that we used in Chapter 6 to describe product and process innovation to introduce the concepts of safety and of product liability risk.

I distinguish between two aspects of the product that can affect consumer willingness to pay. The first is product safety, which we indicate with $\theta_S$. The second dimension includes other aspects of product quality, which we indicate with $\theta_O$. In the case of automobiles, these other factors may comprise car speed, comfort, design, etc. We also extend the model, assuming that each unit of product sold, $q$, may fail with probability $\rho$, in which case the firm will have to pay damages, $D$. In this extended model, the profits of the firm can be written as

$$\pi = p(\theta_S, \theta_O, q)q - (c + \rho D)q$$

where, as in Chapter 6, $q$ is the quantity of product sold, $p(\theta_S, \theta_O, q)$ is the price (increasing in $\theta_S$ and $\theta_O$ and decreasing in $q$) and $c$ is the per-unit cost of production.

Inspecting this formula, it is easy to see the two effects of an RMT: it increases $\theta_S$ and it reduces $\rho$. On the one hand, RMTs create value by increasing consumers' willingness to pay because products are now safer. On the other hand, safer products reduce firms' product liability costs, which is equivalent to a reduction in production costs. By acting simultaneously on $\theta_S$ and $\rho$, an RMT behaves both as a product innovation and as a cost-reducing process innovation.

A final important difference between RMTs and technologies affecting other dimensions of quality is that the value created by RMTs is strongly influenced by non-market forces. Consider, for example, the development of a new pedestrian detection system for cars, which alerts drivers of pedestrians on their path. The profits that an innovator can make will depend on the existing regulations on car safety (will the device become a mandated safety feature?), on the liability system (how large are the damages in case of a collision with a pedestrian?) as well as on the media attention on the subject and on the level of consumer activism. Moreover, the efficiency of the insurance markets that can protect against the risk will also shape the market potential of a risk mitigating technology.[11]

## 8.5 Managing Product Liability Risk through Innovation: A Strategic Approach

In Section 8.4, I argued that RMTs generate value through two distinct, but related, channels. The first is consumers' willingness to pay. RMTs lead to safer products, which generate benefits to customers. The second mechanism by which RMTs create value is by reducing firms' product liability costs. Recognizing these two channels is important because it suggests that RMTs may differ across these dimensions. Building on this insight, Hong Luo and I have developed a framework that identifies different types of RMTs and can help technology strategists to effectively manage these innovations.[12]

To classify their RMTs, managers should assess several aspects of the technology. The first issue to consider is whether the new technology increases consumers' willingness to pay and whether the increase can be translated into greater product market profits. We refer to this dimension as the *product market effect* of the technology.

Managers should then assess the impact of the technology on product liability litigation. RMTs potentially reduce the exposure of firms to liability risk in two ways. They may decrease the likelihood of being involved in litigation; they may also reduce the litigation costs and damages that firms expect to face if litigation takes place.

Defensive effect

|  | | LOW | HIGH |
|---|---|---|---|
| Product market effect | LOW | Ineffective RMT | Defensive RMT |
|  | HIGH | Differentiating RMT | Core RMT |

**Figure 8.1.** A taxonomy of RMTs

Source: Galasso, A., & Luo, H. (2023). Managing medical device liability through innovation: A strategic approach. *Health Management, Policy and Innovation*, 8(1), Figure 1. https://hmpi.org/2023/06/09/managing-medical-device-liability -through-innovation-a-strategic-approach/

The framework Hong Luo and I developed labels this aspect the *defensive effect* of RMTs.

Figure 8.1 illustrates a taxonomy of RMTs depending on their defensive and product market effects. *Ineffective RMTs* are technologies that are not expected to have much success with consumers (low product market effect) and are unlikely to improve the legal position of the firm in product liability litigation (low defensive effect). These RMTs are unlikely to generate value, and managers may prefer not to develop them.

*Defensive RMTs* are technologies with high defensive effect and low product market effect. These are devices that substantially improve a firm's legal position but that consumers do not like because the safety features impact other characteristics of the product in ways that reduces customer satisfaction. For example, installing a speed limiter on a motorcycle reduces the likelihood of serious accidents, but also reduces the pleasure that some consumers derive from reaching high speed.

Childproof prescription drug containers are another example of defensive RMTs. These technologies can protect pharmaceutical companies and pharmacies against product liability litigation because they reduce the chances that children access and swallow unprescribed medicines. For example, in 2018 the US Department of Justice successfully prosecuted a claim against the pharmaceutical firm Dr. Reddy's Laboratories related to the distribution of prescription drugs in blister packs that were not child resistant. Despite the beneficial effects of these technologies, survey evidence shows that adults are dissatisfied with these containers and find them too hard to open. This is especially the case for the elderly and people with disabilities.[13] In the context of CT scanners and other diagnostic technologies, defensive RMTs include readiness-check software, which prevents operators from using a device until a series of quality assurance checks are satisfied. These RMTs reduce the risk of equipment malfunction but can also slow down clinical workflow and reduce the number of patients that hospitals can serve.

*Differentiating RMTs* are technologies with high product market effects and low defensive effects. They are valued by customers but can be challenging to defend in product liability litigation. These are typically technologies that depart substantially from the more established designs in the product market.

An example of differentiating RMTs are robotic surgery systems. Robotic surgery can generate large safety benefits by allowing greater precision during surgical operations and by reducing post-operative complications and recovery time. At the same time, during the past decade surgical robot companies, such as Intuitive Surgical, have been the target of substantial product liability litigation. In some of these cases plaintiffs have alleged that components in the arms of robotic systems caused severe burns to healthy tissues and organs.[14] This litigation is complex and uncertain because it is difficult to determine whether the undesirable outcome was caused by the surgeon, the design of the robotic device, or both. The rapid evolution of the technology makes robotic system manufacturers easier targets of design defect lawsuits relative to other medical device firms that operate in fields where decades-old safety standards are in place.

It is not uncommon for radical technologies capable of reducing injuries and preventing deaths to face commercialization challenges due to the threat of product liability. This happened with the first airbag device, which was developed in United States in the 1960s. In the 1970s, many consumer advocates were calling for adoption of the technology by car manufacturers, but the industry appeared reluctant to install airbags in vehicles. Scholars have argued that product liability litigation was an important reason behind the slow diffusion of the technology. Manufacturers worried that fitting airbags in older models of car not designed to have an airbag would lead to more injuries to drivers. Another concern was that airbags would not fire in some collisions, especially those in which the car speed was low, and this would have affected consumers' perception of the safety of the car.[15]

*Core RMTs* are technologies that provide legal protection and high customer value in tandem. An example of this type of RMT is *Saw-Stop*, a sensor designed to stop a saw blade almost instantly after it hits human flesh. The technology has the potential to avoid substantial numbers of injuries; every year thousands of people suffer amputations using table saws. In fact, the Consumer Product Safety Commission is considering the creation of a mandatory standard requiring all table saws to include this sensing device. There is substantial consumer value in this technology, and its adoption would definitely strengthen table-saw producers' position in product liability suits. Another example of core RMT is the coffee-cup sleeve, which spread rapidly after a jury awarded a McDonald's customer $2.86 million for injuries she suffered from spilling hot coffee.

In the medical device sector, an example of core RMTs is the iterative reconstruction (IR) imaging technique in CT scanners. IR allows for large levels of radiation dose reduction (up to 80–90 percent) in CT scanners relative to other imaging methods. This reduces the risk of patient over-radiation and its associated litigation risk. GE's product brochure for one of its CT scanners using the IR algorithm displays the following message in large font: "'The breakthrough that is rewriting the rule of CT imaging,' and [it] adds that this technology helps physicians to achieve 'the enhanced image quality at a radiation dose never before thought possible.'"[16]

The development of core RMTs is a key driver of competitive advantage for some companies. The Swedish car manufacturer Volvo is an example of a firm that placed risk-mitigation at the center of its technology strategy. The corporate philosophy is well capture by this statement from co-founder Gustaf Larson: "Cars are driven by people – the guiding principle behind everything we make at Volvo, therefore, is and must remain safety."[17] The company has been a leader in the development of safety technologies since 1959 when it became the first car producer to provide three-point safety belts as standard.

Another company perceived as a leader in safety is the medical device firm Becton Dickinson (BD). Incorrect use and disposal of syringes can expose patients and healthcare workers to risk from bloodborne pathogens, such as HIV and hepatitis C. To address this concern, BD developed a variety of technologies, such as syringes with retractable needles, pivoting needles, and shielding needles. The success obtained with these devices led the firm to focus its entire technology strategy around healthcare worker safety.[18]

Productive research programs can yield a mixture of core, differentiating, and defensive RMTs. Core RMTs tend to create the most value, and often they are the easiest to commercialize. In the case of defensive and differentiating RMTs, firms can develop strategies to compensate for low customer values or low liability effects. In other words, companies can try to transition their non-core RMTs into core RMTs.

After the development of defensive RMTs, firms may complement the commercialization of the technology with an information campaign in which product risks are explained to consumers and the general public. Johnson & Johnson, a technology leader in child-proof containers, is also a founding sponsor of "Safe Kids Worldwide," a nonprofit organization that aims at preventing children injuries through the development of information campaigns on safe medicine storage.

In the case of differentiating RMTs, firms should try to convince other firms in the industry to adopt the technology. The more a differentiating RMT becomes a standard feature in the industry, the lower the liability risk associated with its novel and unique design. In the case of the airbag, Mercedes-Benz and Ford played a crucial role in coordinating the leading car manufacturers to adopt the technology. Mercedes-Benz developed a leadership position in the technology area by selling airbags in Europe. Ford showed its commitment to the technology by being the only manufacturer willing to bid on a government contract to equip 5,000 cars for public agencies with airbags in 1983. Both of these moves have been described as key forces that pushed the industry to adopt the technology in the late 1980s.[19]

## 8.6  Product Liability and the Vertical Chain

Product liability risk can affect innovation incentives of firms by shaping their interactions with suppliers and distributors. A good illustration of this phenomenon is the litigation that took place in the 1990s in the US medical implant device industry.

Medical implants are medical devices placed inside or on the surface of the human body. Often, implants replace body parts (in this case they are called "prostheses") but there are also implants that deliver medication, monitor body functions, or provide support to organs and tissues. Classic examples of implants are artificial hips, silicone breast implants, and artificial heart valves. Implants are produced using "biomaterials," which are materials capable of being in contact with the human body for a prolonged period. Most biomaterials are common metals, polymers, or ceramics and are often produced and distributed by large companies that supply a wide range of industrial sectors.

The firm Vitek was the leading manufacturer of artificial jaw (temporomandibular joint) implants in the 1980s. Its product was approved by the FDA and well received by oral surgeons across the United States. In the late 1980s, unexpected and widespread problems arose with Vitek's implants. Some of these devices disintegrated in the body and this led to pain and suffering for numerous patients. The injured patients started litigation with Vitek, but the company was cash constrained and filed for bankruptcy quickly, leaving essentially no compensation for the plaintiffs. Following Vitek's bankruptcy, the lawyers for the patients filed a large number of lawsuits against DuPont, the raw material supplier for Vitek's implants. DuPont was seen as a big corporation with substantial cash flow, and the hope was to obtain some form of compensation for their clients. Eventually, DuPont won (or settled) all the lawsuits, but the process took ten years and cost over $40 million. In contrast, DuPont's revenue from selling material to the TMJ implant producer was only a few thousand dollars.[20]

These events were a big shock to the industry. For decades, suppliers of biomaterials sold their products to medical device producers not expecting any liability risk. The DuPont litigation changed this perception, and suppliers of materials to producers of permanent implants started worrying about litigation from medical device users.

This led many suppliers to drastically change their supply policies. DuPont refused to sell biomaterials to all manufacturers of permanently implantable medical devices. Their supply policy for nonimplant devices remained unchanged. Several other major suppliers also followed DuPont's strategy around the same time. A 1995 report on the status of the biomaterial market documented that roughly 60 percent of polymer suppliers were unwilling to sell to producers of medical implants.[21] The fear of product liability suits was found to be the primary reason for the market foreclosure.

In research with Hong Luo, we examine how this surge in liability risk faced by upstream input suppliers affected innovation incentives for downstream implant producers. Because the supply policies for nonimplant medical devices did not change, the study uses nonimplant medical devices as a comparison group to account for common trends in innovation incentives of the medical device industry more generally.[22]

The statistical analysis shows, overall, a substantial decrease in the number of new patents related to implantable medical devices in the five years after Vitek's bankruptcy in 1990. The drop in innovation in medical implants patenting appears linked to device producers' expectation of a supply shortage of material inputs.[23]

To address this problem, in 1998, the US Congress enacted a new piece of legislation, the Biomaterial Access Assurance Act (BAAA). This act exempted biomaterial suppliers from liabilities as long as they were not involved in the design, production, or distribution of implants. This reduced the litigation risk perceived by suppliers and restored input access to downstream manufacturers. Indeed, patenting output of implant manufactures recovered after 1998, which suggests that this policy helped reestablish innovation incentives.

The Dupont litigation is an important case study illustrating one situation in which liability risk may negatively affect innovation incentives. Of particular note, the increased liability risk had no impact on DuPont's patenting. Instead, the effect of liability risk percolated throughout the vertical chain, suppressing innovation in a downstream sector.

There are a few key features of the business environment that played an important role in generating the supply shortage and in affecting innovation through this channel. First, a critical input was supplied by large multimarket firms with deep pockets, which were able to foreclose a risky downstream segment. Second, downstream innovators were small and likely to resort to bankruptcy when liability claims exceeded firm values. Third, there were sufficient informational frictions (including asymmetric information and uncertainty over the likelihood of product failures and the extent of harms) and transactions costs such that it was hard for downstream producers to be fully insured and for the parties to write contracts that could allocate liability.

These conditions are not uncommon. They hold in several important and innovative industries, such as healthcare, transportation, and energy. The first condition is very prevalent in the case of mass-produced general-purpose inputs, such as semiconductor chips, engines, and batteries. These features are also present in the artificial intelligence (AI) sector. Because of economies of scale and scope, many AI software and data providers are big firms supplying to many heterogeneous markets. Concerns about liability risk may make them reluctant to supply to some particular AI applications. This may not slow down innovation in (upstream) AI software but may substantially affect the development of (downstream) technologies related to the specific application.

# Concluding Remarks

The frameworks and the research insights presented across the chapters of this book have several implications for managers who seek to promote innovation in their organizations. In these concluding remarks, I highlight three general lessons drawn from my analysis of the literature on the economics and management of innovation. The first two emerge as natural conclusions from the discussions of technology management and creation developed in the book. The last one comes from the broader literature examining the welfare benefits and costs associated with the innovation process.

## Lesson 1: Recognize the Value of IP

Many small and medium-sized firms tend to neglect, or to underplay, the role of intellectual property when they develop their business and technology strategies. Sometimes, this is because of the costs associated with filing and maintaining IP. In other cases, the massive legal expenses required to enforce IP rights may induce firms to perceive them as tools that are relevant only for large firms. Even within large corporations, IP is sometimes seen as an issue for lawyers, not crucial for engineers and scientists conducting R&D, and even less relevant for other areas of business management.

One important implication of the material presented in the first part of the book is that IP should play a key role in the technology strategies of firms, small and large alike. IP is not simply a legal tool useful to block imitators. IP rights are crucial assets that firms should manage as effectively as possible. They can be used to prevent other firms from accessing key technologies, but they can also facilitate sharing of technologies through licensing contracts. IP assets can be used as collateral for debt financing and provide important signals of value to potential investors.

Our discussion has also emphasized the richness of the information contained in patent data. Patent databases are free to access and include massive amounts of records. This information can be extremely useful for conducting an analysis of the competitive and technological landscape in which a firm operates. A final implication of our analysis is the value of IP education. Employees across all the various layers of the organization may benefit from knowing the types of IP rights available to the firm, and from understanding their costs and benefits.

## Lesson 2: Understand the Plurality of Innovation Drivers

The academic literature exploring the drivers of innovation is vast and intimidating. Moreover, most of the research tends to focus on the measurement of specific mechanisms in isolation whereas, in practice, multiple channels often overlap and interact, offsetting or reinforcing each other. The goal of the second part of the book was not to provide a complete review of all the studies in the literature but to present several relevant channels – internal and external to the organization – that may shape the level and the direction of R&D investments.

An important implication of our analysis is that innovation is a complex phenomenon that is affected by a large number of variables.

Internally, factors such as corporate culture, executive vision, work-force composition, and compensation schemes play crucial roles. Externally, competitive pressures at the industry and geographical levels, consumer preferences, and government regulation are also fundamental drivers of innovation. The general lesson from the literature surveyed is that managers may benefit from re-assessing the technology strategy of a firm when they observe substantial changes within their organization or in the competitive and regulatory environment in which their firm operates.

## Lesson 3: Keep in Mind Both the Bright and the Dark Sides of Innovation

Throughout this book, I emphasized the beneficial effects of innovation. Technological breakthroughs generate massive entrepreneurial opportunities, and established firms can rely on innovation to preserve their competitive advantage. The benefits of innovation are much broader than their impact on firms' profits and economic growth. New discoveries can improve public health, save lives, and improve the quality of life. However, these massive beneficial effects are not the only reasons why new technologies are central to policy debates. In many circumstances, technological progress also has negative impacts. Well-informed policy and managerial decisions require an understanding of these negative effects and the possible trade-offs they generate. Take, for example, the technological developments that led to modern industrial production processes. These technologies spurred greater production of goods and generated an increase in per-capita income. At the same time, these very same technologies had negative impacts on the environment, leading to climate change and pollution.

Technological progress can also have dramatic impacts on employment. At least since the Luddite movement of the eighteenth century, workers have worried about machines replacing their jobs. These worries have intensified in recent years, as technological developments in the field of artificial intelligence (AI) have sparked several public debates on what jobs will be affected by the new technologies and how.

Historically, leading economic thinkers, such as Keynes and Leontief, predicted widespread technological unemployment as manufacturing equipment diffused. Leontief, in particular, drew an analogy with the technologies of the early twentieth century that made horses redundant. In an interview he stated:

> *Labor will become less and less important ... More and more workers will be replaced by machines. I do not see that new industries can employ everybody who wants a job.*[1]

These predictions did not come true. Recent advances in economic theory can explain why negative effects on employment and wages are not the only possible effects of innovation on jobs. Research by economists Daron Acemoglu and Pascual Restrepo shows that the introduction of new technologies can generate short-term unemployment, but this can be compensated by long-term job creation as innovation generates new types of occupations.[2] The history of the Industrial Revolution provides support to this idea and shows that new technologies that initially replaced workers led to the creation of entirely new job categories. As described by economic historian Joel Mokyr:

> *The sons and daughters of the handloom weavers, nailmakers, and framework knitters found employment as railroad engineers, electricians, telegraph operators, department store clerks, and other occupations that were not imaginable by their parents.*[3]

To conclude, innovation is a key engine of economic growth, with tremendous beneficial effects on firm competitiveness and welfare. At the same time, diffusion of new technologies may also generate pollution, unemployment, and other social costs. While this book has focused on the beneficial effects that technology has on firms and their profits, it is important to keep in mind the broader trade-offs associated with innovation and technological progress.

# Appendix: An Example of Patent Landscape Analysis

In this appendix, I present a simple patent analytics report that applies some of the key concepts discussed in Chapter 3. To conduct this exercise, I consider the case of an inventor who has developed a new foldable sofa-bed and would like to learn more about the technology area of the invention. Below, I collect a dataset of patents granted by the USPTO on related technologies and provide some insights on the innovation trends and the key players active in this research area, and I identify the most valuable patents.[1]

## A.1 The Sample: Foldable Sofas Patents

I begin the analysis by identifying all the patents with primary CPC classification in the subclasses A47C17/23, A47C17/22, and A47C17/225 granted by the USPTO during the years 2010–19. These subclasses were chosen after reading their descriptions on the USPTO portal. They appear as a natural fit for foldable sofa-beds because they capture patents related to seating furniture:

*having non-movable back-rest changeable to beds with means for uncovering a previously hidden mattress or similar bed part* (A47C 17/22);

*with hidden separate full size mattress frame unfolded out of the base frame* (A47C 17/225);

*with the lying down bed surface partly consisting of one side of the seat* (A47C 17/23).

In addition, for each of the patent documents in these classes, I identify the patents that Google Patents highlights as "related patents." I read the title and the abstract of these patents and include in our sample those that appear related to sofas that can be converted into a bed. Finally, I perform a series of keyword searches on Google Patents, using the terms "sofa convertible into bed," "sofa bed," "sofa sleeper" to identify additional patent documents.

The final sample comprises 53 utility patents granted by the USPTO during the years 2010–19.

## A.2 Patenting over Time

As a first step in our analysis, I examine how patenting activity in the technology area has evolved over time during our sample period. Figure A.1 plots the number of patents applied for in each year between 2003 and 2017. There is a steady increase in applications during the period 2003–2010, followed by a drop and a second wave of patenting for the period 2011–14. A second drop is observed in the period 2014–17.

To observe a drop at the end of the sample period is natural in most patent analytics analysis that rely on recent data. In our exercise, the drop takes place because the sample includes only patents granted before 2020 (the year in which I conducted the analysis). Many patents that are filed during the last years of the sample period are likely to still be under review and not granted by 2020, and therefore are excluded from the sample. Technically, this issue is called a truncation problem. Notice that truncation may also affect

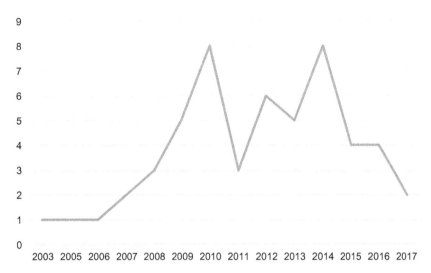

**Figure A.1.** Patenting applications per year

the beginning of the sample period, because patents filed in 2003 or 2004 may have been granted before 2010 so they are not included in the sample.

   Overall, Figure A.1 does not provide strong evidence of a clear trend in patent applications. There is not a steady increase nor a steady decrease in patent applications over the entire time window. Rather, I observe small fluctuations over time, which are consistent with the idea that research investments in the technology area were relatively constant during our sample period.

## A.3 Top Assignees and Inventors

I now turn to the analysis of patent ownership. Overall, there are more than 30 distinct assignees active in this technology field. Most of these patentees own only one or two sample patents. Table A.1 lists the five largest patentees in our data.

Table A.1. Top assignees

| Patents | Assignee |
| --- | --- |
| 7 | Ultra-Mek, Inc. |
| 5 | Lippert Components Manufacturing, Inc. |
| 4 | Cozy Comfort, LLC. |
| 4 | Louis Rodriguez |
| 3 | Flexsteel Industries, Inc. |

Table A.2. Most prolific inventors

| Inventor | Number of Patents |
| --- | --- |
| Marcus L. Murphy | 8 |
| Louis Rodriguez | 4 |
| Jerry A. Thurow | 3 |
| Joseph Cabrera | 3 |
| W. Clark Rogers, Jr. | 3 |

Even the largest patent owner has only seven patents, which is a relatively small patent portfolio relative to other technology areas in which firms file dozens of patents each year. In terms of industry concentration, the top three patentees together own sixteen patents, which is about 30 percent of the sample. This is a nontrivial share of patenting, which suggests some level of concentration but not as high as other technology areas. For example, a report by WIPO indicates that Nokia owns 33 percent of the standard essential patents for Global System for Mobile Communication (GSM) technologies, and that the top three players in the field account for more than 50 percent of these standard essential patents.[2]

Table A.2 lists the top inventors in our sample. Interestingly, the inventor with the largest number of patents has more patents than the top assignee. This is because the person is listed on patents filed by different firms. As in the case of the assignees, the number of inventors in our sample is quite large and the innovation activity does not appear to be entirely driven by only a handful of individuals.

Table A.3. Patent location throughout the world

| Assignee Location | Number of Patents |
|---|---|
| United States of America | 46 |
| Belgium | 1 |
| Brazil | 1 |
| China | 2 |
| France | 1 |
| Italy | 2 |
| Total | 53 |

Table A.4. Patent location in the United States of America

| Assignee Location | Number of Patents |
|---|---|
| California | 11 |
| Florida | 2 |
| Iowa | 3 |
| Indiana | 6 |
| Missouri | 1 |
| Mississippi | 1 |
| North Carolina | 13 |
| Nevada | 1 |
| New York | 1 |
| Ohio | 1 |
| Pennsylvania | 2 |
| Texas | 2 |
| Washington | 1 |
| Wisconsin | 1 |
| Total | 46 |

Tables A.3 and A.4 describe the geographical location of the assignees in our sample. From a global perspective, the United States appears to be the leading source of patenting (not surprising given that the sample only includes USPTO patents). Other areas in which I observe some patenting include Belgium, Brazil, China, France, and Italy. Table A.4 describes the locations within the United States. North Carolina and California appear to be the two states accounting for the largest number of innovating firms operating in the field.

Table A.5. Highly cited patents

| Patent Number | Citations Received by July 2021 | Application Year | Citations Received per Year |
|---|---|---|---|
| 9,009,896 | 27 | 2012 | 3 |
| 9,468,304 | 20 | 2014 | 2.85 |
| 8,881,325 | 20 | 2012 | 2.22 |
| 8,997,273 | 17 | 2013 | 2.12 |
| 8,438,676 | 24 | 2009 | 2 |
| 8,225,439 | 20 | 2011 | 2 |

## A.4 Impactful Patents

The next step in our analysis is to retrieve the number of citations received by each patent in the sample. I then identify the patents that have received more lifetime citations.

A possible concern in comparing the total citations received by each patent is that some of the patents in our sample were filed much earlier than others. In this case, the larger number of citations could simply be mechanically driven by the age of the patent. To address this concern, I computed not only the total citations received by the patents (by July 2021) but also the citations received per year by each patent since the patent application. Table A.5 reports the six patents with the highest number of citations per year.

The data show that patent 9,009,896 filed in 2012 by the American firm Pragma Corporation is the one that scores highest both in terms of total lifetime citations and citations per year. A number of other patents also appear influential in the field, receiving more than twenty total citations and more than two cites per year.

# Notes

## Introduction

1 Quoted in Abbott, A. (2009). Neuroscience: One hundred years of Rita. *Nature, 458,* 564–7. https://doi.org/10.1038/458564a
2 Isaacson, W. (2011). *Steve Jobs.* Simon & Schuster.
3 The title of the blog post alluded to an internet meme catchphrase popular at the time: "All Your Base Are Belong to Us."
4 Google Patent Search™ service is a trademark of Google LLC and this book is not endorsed by or affiliated with Google in any way.

## 1. Intellectual Property

1 Quoted in Face value: Blood and oil. (2000, March 4). *The Economist, 354*(8160), 97.
2 Taking intellectual property seriously. (n.d.). Chief Executive. https://chiefexecutive.net/taking-intellectual-property-seriously/
3 Intangible asset market value study. (n.d.). Ocean Tomo. https://www.oceantomo.com/intangible-asset-market-value-study/
4 Landes, W.M., & Posner, R.A. (2009). *The economic structure of intellectual property law.* Harvard University Press.
5 Kaufer, E. (1988). The economics of the patent system. *Fundamentals of Pure and Applied Economics, 30.* Harwood Academic Publishers.
6 Comino, S., Galasso, A., & Graziano, C. (2020). Market power and patent strategies: Evidence from Renaissance Venice. *The Journal of Industrial Economics, 68*(2), 226–69. https://doi.org/10.1111/joie.12223
7 According to Erich Kaufer, the Venetian government was inspired by the privileges granted in Tyrol (a region of Austria) to those who devised

"Wasserkuenste," that is, mechanical draining machines to draw ground water from mining areas. See Kaufer. The economics of the patent system.

8  Kaufer (1988).

9  Coleman, M. (1976). The Canadian patent office from its beginnings to 1900. *Bulletin of the Association for Preservation Technology*, 8(3), 56–63. https://doi.org/10.2307/1493571

10  Kostylo, J. (2008). Commentary on the Venetian decree of 1545 regarding author/printer relations. In L. Bently & M. Kretschmer (Eds.), *Primary sources on copyright (1450–1900)*. https://www.copyrighthistory.org/cam /tools/request/showRecord.php?id=commentary_i_1545

11  Gans, J.S., & Stern, S. (2003). The product market and the market for "ideas": Commercialization strategies for technology entrepreneurs. *Research Policy*, 32(2), 333–50. https://doi.org/10.1016/S0048-7333(02)00103-8. The original work by Arrow is Arrow, K. (1962). Economic welfare and the allocation of resources for invention. In Nelson, R.R. (Ed.), *The rate and direction of inventive activity: Economic and social factors* (pp. 609–26). Princeton University Press.

12  Cockburn, I.M. (2006). Is the pharmaceutical industry in a productivity crisis? *Innovation Policy and the Economy*, 7, 1–32. https://doi.org/10.1086 /ipe.7.25056188

13  Gambardella, A., Harhoff, D., & Nagaoka, S. (2011). *The social value of patent disclosure* [Unpublished manuscript]. LMU Munich.

14  The quote is from Hopenhayn, H., Llobet, G., and Mitchell, M. (2006). Rewarding sequential innovators: Prizes, patents, and buyouts. *Journal of Political Economy*, 114(6), 1041–68. https://doi.org/10.1086/510562

15  Farre-Mensa, J., Hegde, D., & Ljungqvist, A. (2020). What is a patent worth? Evidence from the US patent "lottery." *The Journal of Finance*, 75(2), 639–82. https://doi.org/10.1111/jofi.12867

16  Galasso, A., & Schankerman, M. (2010). Patent thickets, courts, and the market for innovation. *The RAND Journal of Economics*, 41(3), 472–503. https://doi.org/10.1111/j.1756-2171.2010.00108.x

17  Murray, F., Aghion, P., Dewatripont, M., Kolev, J., & Stern, S. (2016). Of mice and academics: Examining the effect of openness on innovation. *American Economic Journal: Economic Policy*, 8(1), 212–52. https://doi .org/10.1257/pol.20140062

18  The steam-engine patent of James Watt is another example of a patent that, according to many historians, reduced the speed of improvements of the underlying technology. See, for example, the discussion in Boldrin, M., & Levine, D.K. (2008). *Against intellectual monopoly* (Vol. 9). Cambridge University Press.

19  Kitch, E.W. (1977). The nature and function of the patent system. *The Journal of Law and Economics*, 20(2), 265–90. https://doi.org/10.1086/466903

20 Green, J.R., & Scotchmer, S. (1995). On the division of profit in sequential innovation. *The RAND Journal of Economics*, 20–33. https://doi.org/10.2307/2556033

21 See Bessen, J., & Maskin, E. (2009). Sequential innovation, patents, and imitation. *The RAND Journal of Economics*, *40*(4), 611–35, and Galasso, A., & Schankerman, M. (2015). Patents and cumulative innovation: Causal evidence from the courts. *The Quarterly Journal of Economics*, *130*(1), 317–69. https://doi.org/10.1111/j.1756-2171.2009.00081.x

22 See Galasso and Schankerman (2015); and Williams, H.L. (2017). How do patents affect research investments? *Annual Review of Economics*, *9*, 441–69. https://doi.org/10.1093/qje/qju029

23 This has been shown to be an important reason why research incentives in early-stage cancer treatments and cancer prevention are more limited than those in late-stage cancer treatments. I discuss this study in more detail in Chapter 8. See also Budish, E., Roin, B.N., & Williams, H. (2015). Do firms underinvest in long-term research? Evidence from cancer clinical trials. *American Economic Review*, *105*(7), 2044–85. https://doi.org/10.1257/aer.20131176

24 Buccafusco, C., & Lemley, M.A. (2017). Functionality screens. *Virginia Law Review*, *107*, 1293–377. https://doi.org/10.2139/ssrn.2888094

25 LoPucki, L.M., Warren, E., & Lawless, R.M. (2019). *Secured transactions: A systems approach*. Aspen Publishers.

26 See Li, X., MacGarvie, M., & Moser, P. (2018). Dead poets' property – how does copyright influence price? *The RAND Journal of Economics*, *49*(1), 181–205, as well as Biasi, B., & Moser, P. (2021). Effects of copyrights on science: Evidence from the WWII book republication program. *American Economic Journal: Microeconomics*, *13*(4), 218–60. https://doi.org/10.1111/1756-2171.12223

27 See Oberholzer-Gee, F., & Strumpf, K. (2007). The effect of file sharing on record sales: An empirical analysis. *Journal of Political Economy*, *115*(1), 1–42, and Waldfogel, J. (2012). Music piracy and its effects on demand, supply, and welfare. *Innovation Policy and the Economy*, *12*(1), 91–110. https://doi.org/10.1086/511995

28 Giorcelli, M., & Moser, P. (2020). Copyrights and creativity: Evidence from Italian opera in the Napoleonic age. *Journal of Political Economy*, *128*(11), 4163–210. https://doi.org/10.1086/710534

## 2. Patent Your Idea

1 The source for the claims and the image in Figure 2.1 is Agha Beigi, H., Christopoulos, C., & Sullivan, T.J. (2018). *System for mitigating the effects of a seismic event* (US Patent No. US 9,976,317 B2). US Patent and Trademark

Office. https://image-ppubs.uspto.gov/dirsearch-public/print/downloadPdf/9976317

2  Chen, C.T., & Chen, D.Z. (2016). Who files provisional applications in the United States? *Scientometrics, 107*(2), 555–68. https://doi.org/10.1007/s11192-016-1855-z

3  Idris, K., & Arai, H. (2006). Bioethics and patent law: The case of the onco-mouse. *WIPO Magazine, 4*(2013), 16–17.

4  Seymore, S.B. (2011). Rethinking novelty in patent law. *Duke Law Journal, 60*(4), 919–76.

5  Lipkus, N.B., Mackie, J.E., & Singer, P.A. (2010). Guidance for reconciling patent rights and disclosure of findings at scientific meetings. *Health Research Policy and Systems, 8*(1), article 15. https://doi.org/10.1186/1478-4505-8-15

6  Almeling, D.S. (2004). Patenting nanotechnology: Problems with the utility requirement. *Stanford Technology Law Review, 1*, 1–22.

7  Sampat, B., & Williams, H.L. (2019). How do patents affect follow-on innovation? Evidence from the human genome. *American Economic Review, 109*(1), 203–36. See also Frakes, M.D., & Wasserman, M.F. (2017). Is the time allocated to review patent applications inducing examiners to grant invalid patents? Evidence from microlevel application data. *Review of Economics and Statistics, 99*(3), 550–63. https://doi.org/10.1257/aer.20151398

8  Modigliani, F., Solow, R., Molina, M., Hoffman, R. Friedman, M., Smalley, R., Shull, C., Simon, H.A., North, D., Herschbach, D., Brown, H.C., Lee, D.M., Nathans, D., Osheroff, D., Khorana, H.G., Hauptman, H., Harsanyi, J.C., Berg, P., Kendall, H., ... Friedman, J. (1997). An open letter to the US Senate. 143 Cong. Rec. 7259. https://www.govinfo.gov/content/pkg/CREC-1997-09-11/pdf/CREC-1997-09-11-pt1-PgH7254.pdf

9  Hegde, D., & Luo, H. (2018). Patent publication and the market for ideas. *Management Science, 64*(2), 652–72. https://doi.org/10.1287/mnsc.2016.2622

10  Gans, J.S., Hsu, D.H. & Stern, S. (2008). The impact of uncertain intellectual property rights on the market for ideas: Evidence from patent grant delays. *Management Science, 54*(5), 982–97. https://doi.org/10.1287/mnsc.1070.0814

11  PCT highlights: The international patent system. (n.d.). WIPO. https://www.wipo.int/pct/en/highlights/

12  Delgado, M., Kyle, M., & McGahan, A.M. (2013). Intellectual property protection and the geography of trade. *The Journal of Industrial Economics, 61*(3), 733–62. https://doi.org/10.1111/joie.12027

13  Cockburn, I.M., Lanjouw, J.O., & Schankerman, M. (2016). Patents and the global diffusion of new drugs. *American Economic Review, 106*(1), 136–64. https://doi.org/10.1257/aer.20141482

14 Serrano, C.J. (2010). The dynamics of the transfer and renewal of patents. *The RAND Journal of Economics, 41*(4), 686–708. https://doi.org/10.1111 /j.1756-2171.2010.00117.x

15 Inter alia see Cornelli, F., & Schankerman, M. (1999). Patent renewals and R&D incentives. *The RAND Journal of Economics, 30*(2), 197–213, and Schankerman, M., & Schuett, F. (2022). Patent screening, innovation, and welfare. *The Review of Economic Studies, 89*(4), 2101–48. https://doi.org/10.1093 /restud/rdab073

16 De Rassenfosse, G., & van Pottelsberghe de la Potterie B. (2013). The role of fees in patent systems: Theory and evidence. *Journal of Economic Surveys, 27*(4), 696–716. https://doi.org/10.1111/j.1467-6419.2011.00712.x

17 Hall, B., & MacGarvie, M. (2010) The private value of software patents. *Research Policy, 39*(7), 994–1009. https://doi.org/10.1016/j.respol .2010.04.007

## 3. Patent Analytics

1 Quoted Hansen, H.L. (2019, April 29). Big Data: "In God we trust. All others must bring data." *IBM Nordic Blog.* https://www.ibm.com/blogs /nordic-msp/in-god-we-trust-all-others-must-bring-data/

2 Griliches, Z. (1998). Patent statistics as economic indicators: A survey. In *R&D and productivity: The econometric evidence* (pp. 287–343). University of Chicago Press.

3 Pakes, A., & Griliches, Z. (1980). Patents and R&D at the firm level: A first report. *Economics Letters, 5*(4), 377–81. https://doi.org/10.3386/w0561

4 Google Patent Search™ service is a trademark of Google LLC and this book is not endorsed by or affiliated with Google in any way.

5 Agrawal, A., Gans, J., & Goldfarb, A. (2018). *Prediction machines: The simple economics of artificial intelligence.* Harvard Business Press.

6 Galasso, A., & Luo, H. (2022). When does product liability risk chill innovation? Evidence from medical implants. *American Economic Journal: Economic Policy, 14*(2), 366–401. https://doi.org/10.1257/pol.20190757

7 Moretti, E. (2011). Local labor markets. In D. Card & O. Ashenfelter (Eds.), *Handbook of labor economics* (Vol. 4b, pp. 1237–313). Elsevier.

8 Agrawal, A., Cockburn, I., Galasso, A., & Oettl, A. (2014). Why are some regions more innovative than others? The role of small firms in the presence of large labs. *Journal of Urban Economics, 81*, 149–65. https://doi .org/10.1016/j.jue.2014.03.003

9 More specifically, the figure plots patents adjusted for quality (citations weighted) using a methodology that I will describe in Section 3.7.

10  Akcigit, U., Baslandze, S., & Stantcheva, S. (2016). Taxation and the international mobility of inventors. *American Economic Review, 106*(10), 2930–81. https://doi.org/10.1257/aer.20150237

11  Criscuolo, P., & Verspagen, B. (2008). Does it matter where patent citations come from? Inventor vs. examiner citations in European patents. *Research Policy, 37*(10), 1892–908. https://doi.org/10.1016/j.respol.2008.07.011

12  Trajtenberg, M. (1990). A penny for your quotes: Patent citations and the value of innovations. *The RAND Journal of Economics, 21*(1), 72–187. https://doi.org/10.2307/2555502

13  This is similar to the "impact factor" used to measure the impact of scientific publications. Academic journals with high impact are those receiving a lot of citations from follow-on studies.

14  Hall, B.H., Jaffe, A., & Trajtenberg, M. (2005). Market value and patent citations. *The RAND Journal of Economics, 36*(1), 16–38.

15  Krugman, P. (1991). *Geography and trade*. MIT Press.

16  Jaffe, A.B., Trajtenberg, M., & Henderson, R. (1993). Geographic localization of knowledge spillovers as evidenced by patent citations. *The Quarterly Journal of Economics, 108*(3), 577–98. https://doi.org/10.2307/2118401

17  Bryan, K.A., Ozcan, Y., & Sampat, B. (2020). In-text patent citations: A user's guide. *Research Policy, 49*(4), 103946. https://doi.org/10.1016/j.respol.2020.103946

18  Schwartz, D.L., & Sichelman, T. (2019). Data sources on patents, copyrights, trademarks, and other intellectual property. In P.S. Menell, D.L. Schwartz, & B. Depoorter (Eds.), *Research handbook on the economics of intellectual property law*. Edward Elgar Publishing.

## 4. Patent Litigation and Licensing

1  Quoted in *Application of Heinrich Ruschig, Walter Aumuller, Gerhard Korger, Hans Wagner, Josef Scholz and Alfred Bander*, 379 F.2d 990, 993 (CCPA 1967), https://casetext.com/case/application-of-ruschig-2.

2  There are several high-profile examples of patents whose validity was dubious but that were never invalidated. One of these is the Amazon "one click" shopping patent, granted in 1999, which ran to full term without its validity ever being resolved by the courts. See Schankerman & Schuett, Patent screening, innovation, and welfare.

3  Schankerman, M., & Scotchmer, S. (2001). Damages and injunctions in protecting intellectual property. *The RAND Journal of Economics, 32*(1), 199–220. https://doi.org/10.2307/2696404

4  Kline's (2004) article in the *MIT Technology Review* is available at https://www.technologyreview.com/2004/04/28/232981/patent-litigation-the-sport-of-kings. See also Bessen, J., & Meurer, M.J. (2005). Lessons for

patent policy from empirical research on patent litigation. *Lewis & Clark Law Review, 9*(1), 1–27.

5 See the account of the life of Kearns in Schudel, M. (2005, February 26). Accomplished, frustrated inventor dies. *Washington Post*. https://www .washingtonpost.com/archive/local/2005/02/26/accomplished-frustrated -inventor-dies/57015eb7-46eb-4f9f-bd60-4c0b98961bc0/

6 Somaya, D. (2003). Strategic determinants of decisions not to settle patent litigation. *Strategic Management Journal, 24*(1), 17–38. https://doi.org/10.1002/smj.281

7 Lanjouw, J.O., & Schankerman, M. (2004). Protecting intellectual property rights: Are small firms handicapped? *The Journal of Law and Economics, 47*(1), 45–74. https://doi.org/10.1086/380476

8 Galasso and Schankerman (2015).

9 Cohen, L., Gurun, U.G., & Kominers, S.D. (2016). The growing problem of patent trolling. *Science, 352*(6285), 521–2. See also Cohen, L., Gurun, U.G., & Kominers, S.D. (2019). Patent trolls: Evidence from targeted firms. *Management Science, 65*(12), 5461–86. https://doi.org/10.1126/science.aad2686

10 Chien, C. (2013). Startups and patent trolls. *Stanford Technology Law Review, 17*, 461. https://doi.org/10.2139/ssrn.2146251

11 Hagiu, A., & Yoffie, D.B. (2013). The new patent intermediaries: Platforms, defensive aggregators, and super-aggregators. *Journal of Economic Perspectives, 27*(1), 45–66. https://doi.org/10.1257/jep.27.1.45

12 Scotchmer, S. (2004). *Innovation and incentives*. MIT Press.

13 Leute, K. (2010). Anatomy of a license agreement. *Technology transfer practice manual*. AUTM Publishing

14 Leute (2010).

15 Katz, M.L., & Shapiro, C. (1985). On the licensing of innovations. *The RAND Journal of Economics, 16*(4), 504–20. https://doi.org/10.2307 /2555509

16 Gallini, N., & Wright, B. (1990). Technology transfer under asymmetric information. *The RAND Journal of Economics, 21*(1), 147–60. https://doi .org/10.2307/2555500

17 Arora, A., Fosfuri, A., & Gambardella, A. (2004). *Markets for technology: The economics of innovation and corporate strategy*. MIT Press.

18 Ziedonis, R., & Galasso, A. (2019). Patent rights and innovation: Evidence from the semiconductor industry. In E. Elgar, P. Menell, D. Schwartz, & B. Depoorter (Eds.), *Research handbook on the economics of intellectual property law*. Edward Elgar Publishing.

19 In bargaining theory, this is often referred to as the Best Alternative to a Negotiated Agreement (BATNA), which is the best option for the negotiating party if negotiations fail.

20 Lerner, J. (1995). Patenting in the shadow of competitors. *Journal of Law and Economics, 38*(2), 563–95. https://doi.org/10.1086/467339

21 Hall, B., & Ziedonis, R. (2001). The patent paradox revisited: An empirical study of patenting in the U.S. semiconductor industry, 1979–95. *The RAND Journal of Economics, 32*(1), 101–28. https://doi.org/10.2307/2696400

22 Arora, A., Fosfuri, A., & Gambardella, A. (2004). *Markets for technology: The economics of innovation and corporate strategy.* MIT Press.

23 Kamien, M., & Tauman, Y. (2002). Patent licensing: The inside story. *The Manchester School, 70*(1), 7–15. https://doi.org/10.1111/1467-9957.00280

24 Fershtman, C., & Kamien, M.I. (1992). Cross licensing of complementary technologies. *International Journal of Industrial Organization, 10*(3), 329–48. https://doi.org/10.1016/0167-7187(92)90001-F

25 Gallini, N.T. (1984). Deterrence by market sharing: A strategic incentive for licensing. *American Economic Review, 74*(5), 931–41.

26 Shapiro, C. (2001). Navigating the patent thicket: Cross licenses, patent pools and standard setting. In A. Jaffe, J. Lerner, & S. Stern (Eds.), *Innovation policy and the economy* (Vol. 1). MIT Press.

27 Galasso, A. (2012). Broad cross-license negotiations. *Journal of Economics & Management Strategy, 21*(4), 873–911. https://doi.org/10.1111/j.1530-9134.2012.00348.x

28 Hall and Ziedonis (2011).

29 Ziedonis, R. (2004). Don't fence me in: Fragmented markets for technology and the patent acquisition strategies of firms. *Management Science, 50*(6), 804–20. https://doi.org/10.1287/mnsc.1040.0208

30 Galasso (2012).

31 As quoted in Lerner, J., & Tirole, J. (2004). Efficient patent pools. *American Economic Review, 94*(3), 691–711. https://doi.org/10.1257/0002828041464641

32 Lerner and Tirole (2004).

33 Galasso, A., & Schankerman, M. (2021). *Licensing life-saving drugs for developing countries: Evidence from the medicines patent pool* (Working Paper No. 28545). National Bureau of Economic Research. https://doi.org/10.3386/w28545. See also Wang, L.X. (2022). Global drug diffusion and innovation with the medicines patent pool. *Journal of Health Economics, 85*, 102671. https://doi.org/10.1016/j.jhealeco.2022.102671

34 Moser, P., & Voena, A. (2012). Compulsory licensing: Evidence from the trading with the enemy act. *American Economic Review, 102*(1), 396–427. https://doi.org/10.1257/aer.102.1.396

35 The full statement is available at Merck. (2007, May 4). Merck & Co., Inc. statement on Brazilian government's decision to issue compulsory license for STOCRIN(TM) [Press release]. MarketScreener. https://www.marketscreener.com/quote/stock/MERCK-CO-INC-13611/news/Merck-Co-Merck-Co-Inc-Statement-on-Brazilian-Government-s-Decision-To-Issue-Compulsory-Lice-345271

36  Gans, J., & Stern, S. (2003). The product market and the market for "ideas": Commercialization strategies for technology entrepreneurs. *Research Policy, 32*(2), 333–50. https://doi.org/10.1016/S0048-7333(02)00103-8

37  Trapani, J., & Gibbons, M. (2020). *Academic research and development: Science and Engineering Indicators 2020* (No. NSB-2020-2). National Science Board, National Science Foundation. https://ncses.nsf.gov/pubs/nsb20202

38  Lach, S., & Schankerman, M. (2008). Incentives and invention in universities. *The RAND Journal of Economics, 39*(2), 403–33. https://doi.org/10.1111/j.0741-6261.2008.00020.x

39  Lach and Schankerman (2008).

40  Lach, S., & Schankerman, M. (2004). Royalty sharing and technology licensing in universities. *Journal of the European Economic Association, 2*(2–3), 252–64. https://doi.org/10.1162/154247604323067961

41  Thursby, J.G., Jensen, R., & Thursby, M.C. (2001). Objectives, characteristics and outcomes of university licensing: A survey of major U.S. universities. *Journal of Technology Transfer, 26*(1–2), 59–72. https://doi.org/10.1023/A:1007884111883

42  Hvide, H.K., & Jones, B.F. (2018). University innovation and the professor's privilege. *American Economic Review, 108*(7), 1860–98. https://doi.org/10.1257/aer.20160284

43  Zhu, B. (2020). *Start-ups as buyers in technology markets: Evidence from the bio-pharmaceutical industry* [Doctoral dissertation, University of Toronto]. TSpace. https://hdl.handle.net/1807/97747

44  Serrano, C. (2010). The dynamics of the transfer and renewal of patents. *The RAND Journal of Economics, 41*(4), 686–708. https://doi.org/10.1111/j.1756-2171.2010.00117.x

45  Kottasova, I. (2014, February 19). *Does formula mystery help keep Coke afloat?* CNN. https://edition.cnn.com/2014/02/18/business/coca-cola-secret-formula/index.html

46  Ganglmair, B., & Reimers, I. (2019). *Visibility of technology and cumulative innovation: Evidence from trade secrets laws*. ZEW-Centre for European Economic Research Discussion Paper (No. 19-035). https://doi.org/10.2139/ssrn.3393510

## 5. Inducement Prizes and Open-Innovation Strategies

1  Quoted in Carroll, L. (1971). Alice's adventures in wonderland. Oxford University Press. (Original work published 1865)

2  Historical document from the House of Commons as quoted in Cattani, G., Ferriani, S., & Lanza, A. (2017). Deconstructing the outsider puzzle: The legitimation journey of novelty. *Organization Science, 28*(6), 965–92. https://doi.org/10.1287/orsc.2017.1161

3  Turnbull, H.W., Scott, J.F., Hall, R.A., & Tilling, L. (Eds.). (1959–77). *The Correspondence of Isaac Newton* (Vol. 7, p. 212). Cambridge University Press, as quoted in Cattani et al. (2017).

4  Cattani et al. (2017).

5  Williams, H. (2012). Innovation inducement prizes: Connecting research to policy. *Journal of Policy Analysis and Management, 31,* 752–76. https://doi.org/10.1002/pam.21638

6  Azoulay, P., Graff Zivin, J.S., Li, D., & Sampat, B.N. (2019). Public R&D investments and private-sector patenting: Evidence from NIH funding rules. *Review of Economic Studies, 86*(1), 117–52. https://doi.org/10.1093/restud/rdy034

7  McKinsey. (2009). *"And the winner is ...": Capturing the promise of philanthropic prizes.* McKinsey and Co.

8  Burstein, M., & Murray, F. (2015). Innovation prizes in practice and theory. *Harvard Journal of Law and Technology, 29,* 401–25.

9  Williams (2012).

10  Davies, A. (2017, November 10). Inside the races that jump-started the self-driving car. *Wired Magazine.* https://www.wired.com/story/darpa-grand-urban-challenge-self-driving-car/

11  Lifshitz-Assaf, H. (2018). Dismantling knowledge boundaries at NASA: The critical role of professional identity in open innovation. *Administrative Science Quarterly, 63*(4), 746–82. https://doi.org/10.1177/0001839217747876

12  Williams (2012).

13  Kremer, M., & Glennerster, R. (2004). *Strong medicine: Creating incentives for pharmaceutical research on neglected diseases.* Princeton University Press.

14  Kremer, M., Levin, J., & Snyder, C.M. (2022). Designing advance market commitments for new vaccines. *Management Science, 68*(7), 4786–814. https://doi.org/10.1287/mnsc.2021.4163

15  Williams (2012).

16  The quotes are from Murray, F., Stern, S., Campbell, G., & MacCormack, A. (2012). Grand innovation prizes: A theoretical, normative, and empirical evaluation. *Research Policy, 41*(10), 1779–92. https://doi.org/10.1016/j.respol.2012.06.013

17  Galton, F. (1902). The most suitable proportion between the values of first and second prizes. *Biometrika, 1*(4), 385–90. https://doi.org/10.1093/biomet/1.4.385

18  Moldovanu, B., & Sela, A. (2001). The optimal allocation of prizes in contests. *American Economic Review, 91*(3), 542–58. https://doi.org/10.1257/aer.91.3.542

19  Boudreau, K., Lacetera, N., & Lakhani, K. (2011). Incentives and problem uncertainty in innovation contests: An empirical analysis. *Management Science, 57*(5), 843–63. https://doi.org/10.1287/mnsc.1110.1322

20  Accelerating the future. (n.d.). XPrize. https://www.xprize.org/prizes/auto

21  Murray et al. (2012).

22  Galasso, A., Mitchell, M., & Virag, G. (2018). A theory of grand innovation prizes. *Research Policy, 47*(2), 343–62. https://doi.org/10.1016/j.respol .2017.11.009

23  Kremer, M., & Glennerster, R. (2004). *Strong medicine: Creating incentives for pharmaceutical research on neglected diseases.* Princeton University Press.

24  Kaiser, J. (2013, August 26). XPrize pulls plug on $10 million genomics competition. *Science Magazine.* https://www.science.org/content/article /xprize-pulls-plug-10-million-genomics-competition

25  Galasso, A. (2020). Rewards versus intellectual property rights when commitment is limited. *Journal of Economic Behavior and Organization, 169,* 397–41. https://doi.org/10.1016/j.jebo.2019.11.027

26  Khan, Z. (2022). History matters. In S. Haber & N. Lamoreaux (Eds.), *The battle over patents: History and politics of innovation.* Oxford University Press

27  Chesbrough, H. (2003). *Open innovation: The new imperative for creating and profiting from technology.* Harvard Business Press.

28  King, A., & Lakhani, K. (2013, Fall). Using open innovation to identify the best ideas. *MIT Sloan Management Review, 55,* 41–8.

29  Finley, K. (2019, April 24). The *Wired* guide to open source software. *Wired Magazine.* https://www.wired.com/story/wired-guide-open-source -software/

30  Belenzon, S., & Schankerman, M. (2015). Motivation and sorting of human capital in open innovation. *Strategic Management Journal, 36*(6), 795–820. https://doi.org/10.1002/smj.2284

31  Lerner, J., & Schankerman, M. (2010). *The comingled code: Open source and economic development.* MIT Press.

32  Lerner, J., & Tirole, J. (2005). The scope of open source licensing. *Journal of Law, Economics, and Organization, 21*(1), 20–56. https://doi.org/10.1093 /jleo/ewi002

33  Lerner and Tirole (2005).

## 6. Innovation Incentives

1  Quoted in Trew, R., & Calder, J. (2010). Ideas Are Like Rabbits! *Proceedings of the IEEE, 98*(11), 1795–8.

2  Cohen, W.M., & Klepper, S. (1996). Firm size and the nature of innovation within industries: The case of process and product R&D. *The Review of Economics and Statistics, 78*(2), 232–43. https://doi.org/10.2307/2109925

3  Henderson, R.M., & Clark, K.B. (1990). Architectural innovation: The reconfiguration of existing product technologies and the failure of

established firms. *Administrative Science Quarterly, 35*(1), 9–30. https://doi
.org/10.2307/2393549

4 Arrow (1962).

5 Henderson and Clark (1990).

6 Things are somehow different for junior scholars, who a few years after
their initial appointment receive a careful performance evaluation.
Depending on the outcome of this review, professors are either granted
"tenure," which implies job security, or their employment contract with
the university comes to an end.

7 Lerner, J. (2012). *The architecture of innovation: The economics of creative organizations*. Harvard Business Press.

8 Lerner, J., & Wulf, J. (2007). Innovation and incentives: Evidence from corporate R&D. *The Review of Economics and Statistics, 89*(4), 634–44. https://
doi.org/10.1162/rest.89.4.634

9 Lerner (2012). This source also describes how the engineers received
badges for reaching 10 and 25 patent applications.

10 Manso, G. (2011). Motivating innovation. *The Journal of Finance, 56*(5),
1823–60. https://doi.org/10.1111/j.1540-6261.2011.01688.x

11 Azoulay, P., Graff Zivin, J.S., & Manso, G. (2011). Incentives and creativity:
Evidence from the academic life sciences. *The RAND Journal of Economics,
42*(3), 527–54. https://doi.org/10.1111/j.1756-2171.2011.00140.x

12 Aghion, P., Van Reenen, J., & Zingales, L. (2013). Innovation and institutional ownership. *American Economic Review, 103*(1), 277–304. See also
Ederer, F., & Manso, G. (2013). Is pay for performance detrimental to innovation? *Management Science, 59*(7), 1496–1513. https://doi.org/10.1257
/aer.103.1.277

13 Svenson, O. (1981). Are we all less risky and more skillful than our
fellow drivers? *Acta Psychologica, 47*(2), 143–8; Moore, D., & Cain, D.
(2007). Overconfidence and underconfidence: When and why people
underestimate (and overestimate) the competition. *Organizational
Behavior and Human Decision Processes, 103*(2), 197–213. https://doi
.org/10.1016/0001-6918(81)90005-6

14 The key idea is that observing whether CEOs exercise fully vested stock
options that are high in-the-money can provide useful information on the
beliefs about future performance. Failure to exercise executive options
when the stock price is very high indicates that the executive overesti-
mates the expected returns from holding the stock.

15 Malmendier, U., & Tate, G. (2005). CEO overconfidence and corporate
investment. *The Journal of Finance, 60*(6), 2661–700; Malmendier, U., and
Tate, G. (2008). Who makes acquisitions? CEO overconfidence and the
market's reaction. *Journal of Financial Economics, 89*(1), 20–43. https://doi
.org/10.1111/j.1540-6261.2005.00813.x

16  Galasso, A., & Simcoe, T.S. (2011). CEO overconfidence and innovation. *Management Science, 57*(8), 1469–84. https://doi.org/10.1287/mnsc.1110.1374

17  Fites, D. (1996). Make your dealers your partners. *Harvard Business Review, 74,* 84–95.

18  Barney, J. (1986). Organizational culture: Can it be a source of sustained competitive advantage? *Academy of Management Review, 11*(3), 656–65. https://doi.org/10.2307/258317

19  Pisano, G. (2019). *Creative construction: The DNA of sustained innovation.* PublicAffairs.

20  Cohen, W.M., & Levinthal, D.A. (1990). Absorptive capacity: A new perspective on learning and innovation. *Administrative Science Quarterly, 35*(1), 128–52. https://doi.org/10.2307/2393553

21  Stern, S. (2004). Do scientists pay to be scientists? *Management Science, 50*(6), 835–53. https://doi.org/10.1287/mnsc.1040.0241

22  Azoulay, P. (2002). Do pharmaceutical sales respond to scientific evidence? *Journal of Economics Management Strategy, 11*(4), 551–94. https://doi.org/10.1162/105864002320757262

23  Arora, A., Belenzon, S., & Sheer, L. (2021). Knowledge spillovers and corporate investment in scientific research. *American Economic Review, 111*(3), 871–98. https://doi.org/10.1257/aer.20171742

24  Fabrizio, K. (2009). Absorptive capacity and the search for innovation. *Research Policy, 38*(2), 255–267. https://doi.org/10.1016/j.respol.2008.10.023

25  Cohen, W. (2010). Fifty years of empirical studies of innovative activity and performance. In B.H. Hall & N. Rosenberg (Eds.), *Handbook of the economics of innovation* (Vol. 1, pp. 129–213). https://doi.org/10.1016/S0169-7218(10)01004-X

26  Teece, D. (1986). Profiting from technological innovation: Implications for integration and collaboration. *Research Policy, 15*(6), 285–305. https://doi.org/10.1016/0048-7333(86)90027-2

27  Cohen (2010).

28  Prusa, T.J., Jr., & Schmitz, J.A. (1991). Are new firms an important source of innovation? *Economics Letters, 35*(3), 339–42. https://doi.org/10.1016/0165-1765(91)90155-E

29  Cassiman, B., & Ueda, M. (2006). Optimal project rejection and new firm start-ups. *Management Science, 52*(2), 262–75. https://doi.org/10.1287/mnsc.1050.0458

30  Google. (2004). Founders' IPO Letter. Alphabet. https://abc.xyz/investor/founders-letters/2004-ipo-letter/

31  Aghion, P., Bloom, N., Blundell, R., Griffith, R., & Howitt, P. (2005). Competition and innovation: An inverted-U relationship. *The Quarterly Journal of Economics, 120*(2), 701–28. https://doi.org/10.1093/qje/120.2.701

32  Dorn, D., Hanson, G.H., Pisano, G., & Shu, P. (2020). Foreign competition and domestic innovation: Evidence from US patents. *American Economic Review: Insights, 2*(3), 357–74. https://doi.org/10.1257/aeri.20180481

33  Bloom, N., Draca, M., & Van Reenen, J. (2016). Trade induced technical change? The impact of Chinese imports on innovation, IT and productivity. *The Review of Economic Studies, 83*(1), 87–117. https://doi.org/10.1093/restud/rdv039

34  Dorn et al. (2020).

35  Foster, R. (1988). *Innovation: The attacker's advantage.* Summit Books.

36  Christiansen, C. (1997). *The innovator's dilemma.* Harvard Business School Press.

37  Gans, J. (2016). *The disruption dilemma.* MIT Press. https://doi.org/10.7551/mitpress/9780262034487.001.0001

38  Gans (2016).

39  Cunningham, C., Ederer, F., & Ma, S. (2021). Killer acquisitions. *Journal of Political Economy, 129*(3), 649–702. https://doi.org/10.1086/712506

## 7. Innovation Ecosystems

1  Florida, R. (2002). *The rise of the creative class.* Basic Books.

2  Agrawal, A., & Galasso, A. (2017). Finding the right innovation ecosystem. In J. Gans & S. Kaplan (Eds.), *Survive and thrive: Winning against strategic threats to your business* (p. 135). Dog Ear Publishing.

3  Hwang, V., Desai, S., & Baird, R. (2019, April). *Access to capital for entrepreneurs: Removing barriers.* Kauffman Foundation. https://www.kauffman.org/wp-content/uploads/2019/12/CapitalReport_042519.pdf

4  DiMasi, J.A., Grabowski, H.G., & Hansen, R.W. (2016). Innovation in the pharmaceutical industry: New estimates of R&D costs. *Journal of Health Economics, 47*, 20–33. https://doi.org/10.1016/j.jhealeco.2016.01.012

5  Chen, H., Gompers, P., Kovner, A., & Lerner, J. (2010). Buy local? The geography of venture capital. *Journal of Urban Economics, 67*(1), 90–102. https://doi.org/10.1016/j.jeconom.2009.09.020

6  Bernstein, S., Giroud, X., & Townsend, R.R. (2016). The impact of venture capital monitoring. *The Journal of Finance, 71*(4), 1591–622. https://doi.org/10.1111/jofi.12370

7  Smith, A. (2010). *The wealth of nations: An inquiry into the nature and causes of the wealth of nations.* Harriman House Limited.

8  Bhidé, A. (2009). The venturesome economy: How innovation sustains prosperity in a more connected world. *Journal of Applied Corporate Finance, 21*(1), 8–23. https://doi.org/10.1111/j.1745-6622.2009.00211.x

9   Chatterji, A.K., & Fabrizio, K. (2012). How do product users influence corporate invention? *Organization Science, 23*(4), 971–87. https://doi .org/10.1287/orsc.1110.0675

10  Chatterji, A.K., Fabrizio, K.R., Mitchell, W., & Schulman, K.A. (2008). Physician-industry cooperation in the medical device industry. *Health Affairs, 27*(6), 1532–43. https://doi.org/10.1377/hlthaff.27.6.1532

11  Von Hippel, E. (2006). *Democratizing innovation.* MIT Press.

12  Saxenian, A. (1996). *Regional advantage.* Harvard University Press.

13  Arora, A., Cohen, W.M., & Walsh, J.P. (2016). The acquisition and commercialization of invention in American manufacturing: Incidence and impact. *Research Policy, 45*(6), 1113–28. https://doi.org/10.1016/j .respol.2016.02.005

14  Alcácer, J., & Chung, W. (2014). Location strategies for agglomeration economies. *Strategic Management Journal, 35*(12), 1749–61. https://doi.org /10.1002/smj.2186

15  Marshall, A. (1890). *Principles of economics* (unabridged 8th ed.). Cosimo, 2009.

16  Berkes, E., & Gaetani, R. (2021). The geography of unconventional innovation. *The Economic Journal, 131*(636), 1466–1514. https://doi .org/10.1093/ej/ueaa111

17  Agrawal and Galasso (2017).

18  Belenzon, S., & Schankerman, M. (2013). Spreading the word: Geography, policy, and knowledge spillovers. *Review of Economics and Statistics, 95*(3), 884–903. See also Hausman, N. (2022). University innovation and local economic growth. *The Review of Economics and Statistics, 104*(4), 718–35. https://doi.org/10.1162/rest_a_01027

19  Anders, G. (2016, January 4). Why the "wrong" location can be a startup's hidden strength. *Forbes.* https://www.forbes.com/sites/georgeanders /2016/01/04/why-the-wrong-location-can-be-a-startups-hidden-strength

20  Agrawal, A., & Cockburn, I. (2003). The anchor tenant hypothesis: Exploring the role of large, local, R&D-intensive firms in regional innovation systems. *International Journal of Industrial Organization, 21*(9), 1227–53. See also Greenstone, M., Hornbeck, R., & Moretti, E. (2010). Identifying agglomeration spillovers: Evidence from winners and losers of large plant openings. *Journal of Political Economy, 118*(3), 536–98. https://doi.org/10.1016/S0167 -7187(03)00081-X

21  The source for this number is Cassiman, B., & Ueda, M. (2006). Optimal project rejection and new firm start-ups. *Management Science, 52*(2), 262–75. https://doi.org/10.1287/mnsc.1050.0458

22  Helsley, R.W., & Strange, W.C. (2002). Innovation and input sharing. *Journal of Urban Economics, 51*(1), 25–45. https://doi.org/10.1006/juec.2001.2235

23 Glaeser, E.L., & Kerr, W.R. (2009). Local industrial conditions and entrepreneurship: How much of the spatial distribution can we explain? *Journal of Economics & Management Strategy, 18*(3), 623–63. https://doi.org/10.1111/j.1530-9134.2009.00225.x

24 Agrawal, A., Cockburn, I., Galasso, A., & Oettl, A. (2014). Why are some regions more innovative than others? The role of small firms in the presence of large labs. *Journal of Urban Economics, 81*, 149–65. https://doi.org/10.1016/j.jue.2014.03.003

25 Smith, A. (1937). A*n inquiry into the nature and causes of the wealth of nations*. Random House. (Original work published 1776)

26 Seitz, M., & Watzinger, M. (2017). Contract enforcement and R&D investment. *Research Policy, 46*(1), 182–95. https://doi.org/10.1016/j.respol.2016.09.015

27 Akcigit, U., Baslandze, S., & Stantcheva, S. (2016), Taxation and the international mobility of inventors. *American Economic Review, 106*(10), 2930–81. https://doi.org/10.1257/aer.20150237

28 Galasso, A., Schankerman, M., & Serrano, C.J. (2013). Trading and enforcing patent rights. *The RAND Journal of Economics, 44*(2), 275–312. https://doi.org/10.1111/1756-2171.12020

29 Agrawal, A., Galasso, A., & Oettl, A. (2017). Roads and innovation. *Review of Economics and Statistics, 99*(3), 417–34. https://doi.org/10.1162/REST_a_00619

30 Saxenian, A. (1996). *Regional advantage*. Harvard University Press.

31 Pairolero, N., Toole, A., DeGrazia, C., Teodorescu, M.H., & Pappas, P.A. (2022). Closing the gender gap in patenting: Evidence from a randomized control trial at the USPTO. *Academy of Management Proceedings, 2022*(1), 14401. https://doi.org/10.5465/AMBPP.2022.197. t.

32 Yang, Y., Tian, T.Y., Woodruff, T.K., Jones, B.F., & Uzzi, B. (2022). Gender-diverse teams produce more novel and higher-impact scientific ideas. *Proceedings of the National Academy of Sciences, 119*(36), e2200841119. https://doi.org/10.1073/pnas.2200841119

33 Koning, R., Samila, S., & Ferguson, J.P. (2021). Who do we invent for? Patents by women focus more on women's health, but few women get to invent. *Science, 372*(6548), 1345–8. https://doi.org/10.1126/science.aba6990

34 Bell, A., Chetty, R., Jaravel, X., Petkova, N., & Van Reenen, J. (2019). Who becomes an inventor in America? The importance of exposure to innovation. *The Quarterly Journal of Economics, 134*(2), 647–713. https://doi.org/10.1093/qje/qjy028

35 Damiano, E., Li, H., & Suen, W. (2010). First in village or second in Rome? *International Economic Review, 51*(1), 263–88. https://doi.org/10.1111/j.1468-2354.2009.00579.x

36 Kerr, S.P., & Kerr, W.R. (2011). *Economic impacts of immigration: A survey* [Working Paper No. 16736]. National Bureau of Economic Research. https://doi.org/10.3386/w16736

37  Marinoni, A. (2023, May 22). Immigration and entrepreneurship: The role of enclaves. *Management Science*. Ahead of print publication. https://doi .org/10.1287/mnsc.2023.4776

38  General Electric (GE). (2016, January 13). *GE moves headquarters to Boston* [press release]. https://www.ge.com/news/press-releases/ge-moves -headquarters-boston

## 8. Health, Safety, and Innovation

1  Quoted in Campos Seijo, B. (2016, June 6). Never let a good crisis go to waste. *Chemical & Engineering News*, 94(23), 3-3. https://cen.acs.org /magazine/94/09423.html

2  Stempel, J. (2020, March 27). GM reaches settlement over lost vehicle value from defective ignition switches. *Reuters*. https://www.reuters.com /article/us-gm-settlement-idUSKBN21E3LG/

3  Grennan, M., & Town, R.J. (2020). Regulating innovation with uncertain quality: Information, risk, and access in medical devices. *American Economic Review*, 110(1), 120–61. https://doi.org/10.1257/aer.20180946

4  Budish et al. (2015).

5  Medical device liability cases are often covered by the media because of the pain and suffering those defective products cause. Leading cases include Bayer's birth control devices, St. Jude's implantable cardioverter-defibrillators, Stryker's hip implants, and Covidien's surgical staplers.

6  Bapuji, H., & Beamish, P.W. (2008, March). Avoid hazardous design flaws. *Harvard Business Review*, 86(3), 23–6.

7  Manley, M. (1987, September/October). Product liability: You're more exposed than you think. *Harvard Business Review*, 65(5), 28–40; Morrow, R.M. (1994). Technology issues and product liability. *Product liability and innovation: Managing risk in an uncertain environment*. National Academy of Engineering.

8  Graham, J. (1991). Product liability and motor vehicle safety. In Huber, P.W., & Litan, R.E. (Eds.). *The liability maze: The impact of liability law on safety and innovation*. Brookings Institution Press.

9  Graham (1991).

10  Galasso, A., & Luo, H. (2021a). Risk-mitigating technologies: The case of radiation diagnostic devices. *Management Science*, 67(5), 3022–40. https:// doi.org/10.1287/mnsc.2020.3634

11  Galasso, A., & Luo, H. (2021b, March 23). Risk perception, tort liability, and emerging technologies. *Brookings Institution*. https://www.brookings.edu/ articles/risk-perception-tort-liability-and-emerging-technologies/

12  Galasso, A., & Luo, H. (2023). Managing medical device liability through innovation: A strategic approach. *Health Policy Management and Innovation*,

*8*(1). https://hmpi.org/2023/06/09/managing-medical-device-liability-through-innovation-a-strategic-approach/

13   Thwaites, J. (1999). Practical aspects of drug treatment in elderly patients with mobility problems. *Drugs and Aging, 14*, 105–14. https://doi.org/10.2165/00002512-199914020-00003

14   Fox, M. (2013). *Electrical burns may burst surgical robot's bubble.* NBC News. https://www.nbcnews.com/healthmain/electrical-burns-may-burst-surgical-robots-bubble-6C10321766

15   Mackay, M. (1991) Liability, safety, and innovation in the automobile industry. In Huber, P.W., & Litan, R.E. (Eds.). *The liability maze: The impact of liability law on safety and innovation* (pp. 191–233). Brookings Institution Press.

16   Galasso and Luo (2021a, p. 3034).

17   Volvo. (n.d.). The E.V.A. initiative: *Cars should protect everyone.* Retrieved January 15, 2024 from https://www.volvocars.com/en-ca/v/car-safety/eva-initiative-cars-equally-safe

18   Pisano, G. (2019). *Creative construction.* PublicAffairs.

19   Graham (1991).

20   Galasso and Luo (2022).

21   Aronoff, M. (1995) Market study: Biomaterials supply for permanent medical implants. *Journal of Biomaterials Applications, 9*(3), 205–60. https://doi.org/10.1177/088532829500900303

22   Galasso and Luo (2022).

23   Galasso and Luo (2022).

**Concluding Remarks**

1   Quoted in Acemoglu, D., & Restrepo, P. (2018). The race between man and machine: Implications of technology for growth, factor shares, and employment. *American Economic Review, 108*(6), 1488–1542. https://doi.org/10.1257/aer.20160696

2   Acemoglu and Restrepo (2018).

3   Mokyr, J. (2002). *The gifts of Athena: Historical origins of the knowledge economy.* Princeton University Press.

**Appendix**

1   I would like to thank Sarina Gill for the research assistance in conducting this exercise.

2   The source is World Intellectual Property Organization. (2017). Success in the smartphone industry. In *World Intellectual Property Report 2017: Intangible Capital in Global Value Chains* (pp. 94–131). WIPO. https://www.wipo.int/edocs/pubdocs/en/wipo_pub_944_2017-chapter4.pdf

# Index

Note: The letter *f* following a page number denotes a figure; the letter *t*, a table.